PAWS TO COMFORT

An everyday guide
to learning how you
can help mend our
disconnected world.

To my husband and chief comforter David, who for 25 years has been at my side with unwavering support and belief. I love you more.

New Degree Press

Contact Information
pawstocomfort@inspiringcomfort.com
pawstocomfort.com (http://pawstocomfort.com/)
inspiring comfort.com (http://inspiringcomfort.com/)

ISBN   978-1-64137-210-7   *Paperback*
          978-1-64137-211-4   *Ebook*

Printed in USA

"Watch carefully, the magic that occurs, when you give a person just enough comfort, to be themselves."

— Atticus

CONTENTS

WE ALL HAVE A ROLE TO PLAY
HOW COMFORT SAVES LIVES

By Dr. John Draper, Executive Director of National Suicide Prevention Lifeline and Executive VP of National Networks, Vibrant Emotional Health

I first met Jen Marr after giving a talk at the New York State Suicide Prevention Conference in 2017. As I left the podium, I was drawn to a beautiful golden retriever sitting nearby. I brushed by attendees to find this bundle of golden fur. I walked right over and as I scratched that soft velvety ear, looked up and said "I looooove Golden Retrievers! I have one at home, and they are the best!" Holding the leash of this beautiful dog was Jen Marr who offered, "Who doesn't love Golden Retrievers?"

What is it about our dogs that disarm us, draw us in, pull us out of ourselves and instantly connect us to a sense of comfort and joy? No matter how our world may be falling apart, there is something in our dogs and pets that often keeps us grounded enough to get us through the darkest nights. In my years of suicide prevention work, it's hard to count the number of times that I have heard suicidal persons say that—in spite of their suffering—it is their pet that is keeping them alive.

So again, what is it about our dogs, our pets? As a psychology student, I was instructed in the basic essentials of what constitutes a truly therapeutic relationship, as postulated by the father of Humanistic Psychology, Dr. Carl Rogers. Rogers' three fundamental relationship elements include unconditional positive regard, genuineness and empathy. If I feel that someone cares for me without judgement (unconditional positive regard), who is authentic and honest in his/her reactions to what I say and feel (genuineness), and who seems to understand and appreciate how I feel (empathy), then I will feel safe to be and feel free to strive towards becoming my best self. Research has been clear that the most powerful influence over whether therapy is effective or not is the quality of the therapeutic relationship. Decades of studies continuously point to these three Rogerian principles as the building blocks of an effective therapeutic relationship. In my work to develop national standards for crisis counselors on hotlines, we have also found that these relationship factors are the most important ones in assisting people in suicidal distress. The central value of these principles should come as no surprise to us, really. Unconditional positive regard, genuineness and empathy are also the essential building blocks of a healthy, prosperous parent-child relationship, from infancy onward.

These three elements are also present in my relationship with my Golden Retriever, Max, who loves me no matter how crappy my day is and no matter what I have (or haven't) done, who responds to me as he is, and with an uncanny sense of understanding when I need to be comforted. Jen Marr and the work she is doing helped me understand that, in effect, my dog is an expert in the field of establishing relationships. He creates comfort within and between he and me, and that comfort is an essential component in creating meaningful connections for all of us.

In 2017, Jen founded Inspiring Comfort, Inc., where she began to spread the word about comfort through public speaking appearances, learning programs, toolkits and workshops in a variety of settings. Her passion in this work has been driven by her belief that comfort is critical to promoting more connectedness in our world, and it is an evidence-based skill that can be taught in a simple way. The more Jen and her colleagues promoted their programs and toolkits, the more requests they received. In turn, she realized that she needed a means to provide more comfort skills to more people. As a

> Through this book, you will learn that comfort is at the intersection of compassion, empathy, and being intentional.

result, she began to research and interview experts towards writing the book that you now have in your hands, Paws to Comfort. Through this book, you will learn that comfort is at the intersection of compassion, empathy, and being intentional.

While the actions that create comfort come natural to dogs, they may feel initially awkward to many of us. We are attuned to a fast-paced world where mobile technologies, the unprecedented 24/7/365 prevalence of media and information, competitive performance pressures, and divisive ideologies dominate our everyday experience. In our first 20 years of this century, we are also seeing escalating anxiety, depression and suicide rates, especially among our younger populations. Could teaching comfort in our homes, schools and communities help us overcome our looming cultural "connection deficit disorder?"

Perhaps now is the time to develop skills that require compassionate connections that ultimately awaken our natural empathic response, something that can be suppressed by the harshness of life. In this book, you will learn how to overcome awkwardness and learn the skill of comfort and connection, in ways that are simple, as elemental as our dog lying next to us.

The mental health community and our dear pets can't do it alone. The world needs all of us to know how to connect with those who are struggling too. Perhaps now is the time for us to learn how to Paws to Comfort.

> The world needs all of us to know how to connect with those who are struggling too.

About Dr. John Draper: Dr. Draper has nearly 25 years of experience in crisis intervention and suicide prevention work, and is considered one of the nation's leading experts in crisis contact center practices (hotline, online chat, SMS services, etc.). He oversees all aspects of the federally-funded National Suicide Prevention Lifeline network, which consists of over 160 member crisis centers across the country. Dr. Draper frequently presents at national conferences on subjects related to best practices in crisis intervention and suicide prevention, as well as the use of innovative technologies (text, chat, other online programs, etc.) in helping persons in emotional distress. Dr. Draper also frequently discusses the role of persons with lived experience of suicide (attempt survivors, loss survivors, etc.) in suicide prevention. Dr. Draper has been quoted in The New York Times, ABC News, The New York Post, and TIME magazine among others.

COMFORT 101: HOW TO USE THIS BOOK

STEP 1: **PAUSE**	The moment this book hits your hands and you see the title and picture of the boy with his dog on the pier, you should exhale. PAWS. Step away from the chaotic world we live in and be in the moment of doing something for yourself and others. Turn off the TV, put the phone down, step away from the computer. Breathe. Remember what life is all about. Remember what matters most. You are about to learn a skill that will enable you to make a real difference in peoples lives.
STEP 2: **THINK**	As you journey through this book and learn the skill of comfort, please keep pausing and remembering what dogs can teach us. They are relational creatures like us humans. They put us first. They embrace every day with the simple things in life. Being together, eating, sleeping & playing. They are beautiful teachers of comfort that we can look at every day for inspiration.
STEP 3: **CONSIDER**	Take some time to take perspective on where we are in our world today. What's changed since you were growing up. What good and bad has come out of all of the latest gadgets and gizmos we now have. What is at the root of our divisive and fast paced world. In order to reverse some alarming trends, it's important that we understand them.
STEP 4: **UNDERSTAND**	You may have never thought of comfort being something you can learn. Most of us haven't. So pause and think about that for a moment. You are holding a wonderful tool for understanding and learning. As you read through the section of learning comfort as a skill remember that there are many facets to this skill. Pause and take some time to digest what hits home. You are going to find that you have unique talents and things you enjoy. These will be key to how you move forward with applying this skill.
STEP 5: **APPLY**	The last step is for you to pause and create your own personal comfort response plan. You will come up with strategies for those awkward moments that you find yourself in. You will identify simple things to do when you can't find words to say and you will begin to change your mindset. You will plan for lots of little moments, taking the pressure off your initial response. Focusing more on actions than words. Having your personal road map will make a huge impact on all of those around you who are desperate to know that you care.

LEARNING COMFORT: HOW IT ALL BEGAN

How the trails in my life came together to open my eyes to a growing need for comfort and equipped me to move forward with this work.

Have you ever wondered where the breadcrumbs of your life are leading? I know I have.... I've always questioned why I'm walking this earth at this place and time in history.

And so, it hit me one day that my entire life has left behind tons of little breadcrumbs that offer clues. Laying out what I'm meant to do in life. I believe this with my whole heart.

My sister Renata Bowers, author of the Frieda B. children's book series, believes it, too. In her most recent book, she encourages readers to explore the story they carry inside by considering the combination of three strands in their life: Your story " is the mixture of all that "you love" and "you do", all combined with experiences "unique to you."

This has held true in my own life. It's in the combination of all of these breadcrumbs that has put me on the trail to discovering the significance of comfort in our world.

So let's consider that we have three trails that we walk down:

1. Our "Brain Trail" - What we are good at and what we do – Our minds at work

2. Our "Heart Trail" - Where our hearts lead us and what we love – Our hearts at work

3. Our "Circumstances Trail" - What happens to us in life – Circumstances and experiences at work

These three trails combine to lead to our life's work. For me, my life's work braids

entrepreneurship, tragedy, and a desire to help.

My "Brain Trail" travels down entrepreneurship. I've come to realize that not everyone's mind is consumed with finding the next new idea or improving the ones already here. Every job I've ever done has started with a blank piece of paper. I love to develop projects. Envision them, start them and grow them. Sometimes I've gotten paid, sometimes I didn't and sometimes I lost money trying something

Comforting each other, even with small gestures, benefits us in profound ways.

that didn't work. But it was always about creating something. Making it better. Doing something different. So, I think this skill set totally qualifies as my brain trail.

My "Circumstances Trail" has always traveled through crisis and tragedy zones. Repeatedly throughout my life. My nickname growing up was Disaster Annie - having almost drowned twice, having the Heimlich done on me as I choked on beef stroganoff and being on a first named basis in the ER as they stitched me, cast me and sent me home wrapped up with ice all too frequently. I thought it was all funny, my parents, not so much. If there was a crisis or disaster, I was sure to be nearby. This pattern followed me into adulthood as I found myself living through terrorist attacks in London and Boston, a major flood in Minnesota, 9/11 with my husband working in New York City, a tornado in Wisconsin and the 1989 earthquake in San Francisco.

My "Heart Trail""grew as Disaster Annie increasingly dealt with each new crisis. As each terrible horrible event happened to me and to those around me, I felt an increasing desire to help. My eyes were opened to everyday pain in those who were suffering. I was led to help. It burned in my heart to help. And with each new tragedy, I felt more equipped to help.

It was a breadcrumb on my "Circumstance Trail" that lead to my "full 3 trail merger". Actually, it was more than just a circumstance. It was a furry Golden Retriever with beautiful brown eyes and a heart the size of Texas. And her name is Addie.

I met LCC K-9 Comfort Dog Addie in January 2013 when she was placed at Immanuel Lutheran Church in Danbury, Connecticut, as the first LCC K-9 Comfort Dog on the east coast to help with the recovery efforts after the tragedy at Sandy Hook Elementary in December of

> With each new tragedy, I felt more equipped to help.

2012. The LCC K-9 Comfort Dogs are known nationwide for responding to crisis and disaster situations. These beautiful golden retrievers and their handlers go through extensive training as part of Lutheran Church Charities' (LCC) mission to share the Mercy, Compassion, Presence and Proclamation of Jesus Christ to those who are suffering and in need.

Addie Comfort Dog arrived in Connecticut ready to serve. As I walked her down the halls of Sandy Hook Elementary, I felt woefully inadequate. All I could think was: Who am I to be doing this? I was terrified. What could I do? I thought. What could anyone do in this situation?

But it became apparent rather quickly that Addie instinctively knew what to do. All the time and in every situation. She was a bridge to those hurting and I just showed up and loved and cared and watched and learned.

It was only 3 months after Addie's arrival that I was running in the Boston Marathon and was ½ mile from the finish line when the bombs exploded. I was left feeling stunned, shocked, angry and confused. "What is happening to our world?", was all I could think. It seemed almost incomprehensible that these two events were only months apart from each other. Now what? I asked myself. Addie and other LCC K-9 Comfort Dogs and their handlers were invited to Boston.

They responded bringing comfort, compassion, and love to the community and those impacted, and in this case it included me.

Since these two events, my life has been fully consumed with observing, learning, providing, teaching and on many days needing comfort. My own little comfort lab.

I have spent thousands of hours responding to suicides, drug overdoses, car accidents, cancer, tragedy, illness and sadness. The list of those needing comfort goes on and on. All around us, sadness and sorrow and a culture that has never been more connected, and never more disconnected at the same time. Those in pain sometimes feeling the most isolated of all.

Every time I left broken lives behind after a deployment I wondered what more could I do? There were just so many people wanting more comfort and needing more comfort than could be provided in a short term crisis response. And so I began the program Club Comfort in 2015 as a way to do more. To bring these shattered lives back together and let them know they were not alone.

We started with a simple activity to help participants comfort others. It grew into something much more as we witnessed how occupying their minds to help others became one of their healing mechanisms. This ultimately led to the founding of Inspiring Comfort LLC and our evidence based programming.

This book is a reflection and a mission resulting from these almost 7 years. How the trails in my life came together to open my eyes to a growing need for comfort and equipped me to move forward with this work. It's about how can we continue to find solutions to our comfort crisis by teaching people how to bring more comforting and caring into this world. We have watched as our programs and workshops have created tens of thousands of comforting connections and are realizing that we haven't even touched the tip of the iceberg.

When I look back on all the breadcrumbs of my life thus far, it's beautiful to see how the loving and calm spirit of dogs have brought this all together. Dogs are amazing that's for sure. But they alone can't reach all those in need. The world needs you comforting too.

"LCC K-9 Comfort Dog Ministry is a registered trademark of Lutheran Church Charities. Inspiring Comfort LLC and Paws to Comfort are not affiliated with Lutheran Church Charities or the LCC K-9 Comfort Dogs.

> We are surrounded by sadness, sorrow and a culture that must relearn the skills to support and comfort each other.

"Mack reached for me and I jumped up on the couch next to him and slept pressed up against him for a little while. Mack was the saddest man I had ever met, but he always seemed happier when I saw him. I was doing my job, fulfilling my purpose, providing comfort."

– Bella, "A Dogs Way Home", W. Bruce Cameron"

PART ONE

DOGS AND COMFORT

How dogs comfort when all else fails

Lessons we learn from dogs

Searching for a solution

PAWS TO HOPE:
HOW DOGS COMFORT WHEN ALL ELSE FAILS

He speaketh not; and yet there lies
a conversation in his eyes".

–Henry W. Longfellow

In 2012 Edie* was a beautiful third grader at Sandy Hook Elementary. She loved animals even more than most kids her age, which says a lot. Dogs, chickens, horses, you name it. They were the center of her life.

On the morning of December 14, that all changed. In mere seconds her daydreams of dogs and chickens and horses were shattered. Chaos ensued as an unthinkable tragedy unfolded a wall away from where she hid. Edie survived but emerged consumed by a cloud of darkness and fear. She withdrew, building emotional walls to shield herself. She was 8 years old.

Days and weeks went by where she stayed secluded in her home. While her classmates were returning to school, Edie could not. Time and time again, her mother would try a new approach. Bringing her in late, or for even only a class or two. But Edie would have none of it. And so, she stayed home terrified to walk into a school again.

Three weeks after all the other students had returned to school, a counselor came to me with the idea of involving LCC K-9 Comfort Dog Addie as a way to motivate Edie to come back. Everything else had failed. Could her love of animals help her to return? It was decided that

*not her real name

we would ask Edie if she would please give Addie her water each morning after the other students went to class. We explained to Edie that Addie got very thirsty comforting everyone and needed a helper to make sure she was hydrated.

And so, it went. She agreed and the counselor and I held our breath. The first day back, Edie ever so slowly brought the water bowl in and gently placed it in front of Addie Comfort Dog. And that was it. She only observed. No petting, no talking, no sitting. Only standing and watching. It was painful to see her keep her distance even from Addie in those early days. So tentative and scared. Her trust in anyone and anything shattered. But day by day, it was the loving eyes and soul of a dog that spoke to her when human words could not break through. They had their own understanding, Addie and Edie, and it wasn't too long before the first "pet" happened. Finally, one morning she sat down and touched Addie's back. I think at that moment Addie and I actually looked at each other and shared unheard shouts of joy between us. Soon she

Day by day, the loving eyes and soul of a dog spoke to her when human words could not break through

was diligently showing up each morning to bring Addie water. And on mornings that she was more downcast than normal, we pointed out that Addie's fur got all messed up from so much petting and she could use a good brushing. This seemed to help her "tune back in" and emotionally prepare for the day ahead. Once her canine jobs were done, Addie walked her to class.

It was a few weeks after she was back at school when she walked in especially sad one morning. So, we saw to it that she got extra time brushing Addie and an extra loop around the halls before joining her class. Later this same day Addie visited Edie's classroom. To set the stage: this was a big part of what Addie did those first 6 months after the tragedy. She would visit classrooms and let students in groups of 4-6 sit in a circle around her and pet her. This was not a "let's have fun and play" kind of visit. Rather, it was always during a quiet time and it was used to help re-ground and re-focus the students. Five minutes in a circle with a fluffy golden retriever could do a whole lot to keep kids motivated and focused during those months. In these cases, an LCC K-9 Comfort Dog is trained to just lay down and be a source of comfort. Thousands of hours of training equips these canines to be the best blankets, pillows and huggers on the planet.

Soon it was Edie's turn in the circle. As she sat down, I noticed that she had on an "it's my birthday" sticker. A happy bubbly sticker stuck to her shirt in stark contrast to her mood. Her eyes, as they were earlier that morning, were still downcast. And in this circle on this day, she really wasn't even engaging much with Addie. Just watching with far away eyes. I remember how incredibly sad I felt at that moment to see such sadness on a birthday. Wanting so badly to wave a magic wand and make it all better for her.

But then as if on que, in one swift motion, Addie sat up and went over to Edie and put her nose on Edie's nose. I still get the chills whenever I recall that moment. If there was anything in life that could have helped this child at this time any better, I have yet to think of it. In one instant with one gesture, a Comfort Dog made a child who desperately needed it feel important and loved. Even more telling was the fact that this was not a normal behavior for Addie. I can recall only a few other times in my many years with her, that she broke her "down" command to stand up and walk over to someone hurting.

A smile grew on Edie's face as she hugged Addie. Her eyes being called back to the present, she looked at me and asked, "Do you think Addie did that because I brushed her today?". Fighting back every ounce of the emotional urge to burst out crying, I assured her that of course she was Addie's special friend and Addie wanted to make sure she had a fabulous birthday.

There was a noticeable change in Edie after that encounter. She took her role with Addie more seriously and reciprocated the friendship even more. The day she came to school with her first ever mobile device, she took her first picture with Addie. When she sent her first email, guess who it went to? LCC K-9 Comfort Dog Addie of course. It was as if that nose to nose touch, magically glued together some of Edie's pieces of brokenness. Almost like a magic wand.

Or maybe it's not so magic.

> With one gesture, a dog made a child who desperately needed it feel important and loved

WHAT IS IT THAT OUR PETS DO FOR US?

You don't have to look very far to see how pets benefit our lives. The Human Animal Bond Research Institute (HABRI) partnered with Cohen Research Group to conduct an online survey of 2,000 pet owners. Here's what they found.

86% of pet owners are aware that pets reduce depression

88% of pet owners are aware that pets reduce stress

84% of pet owners were aware that pets reduce anxiety

60% of pet owners were aware that pets improve heart health

80% of pet owners were aware that pets help with conditions like PTSD in war veterans

81% of pet owners are aware that pets increase our sense of well-being

65% of pet owners were aware that pets help with conditions like autism

56% of pet owners were aware that pets help with conditions like Alzheimer's disease

68% of pet owners were aware that pets support healthy aging

THE MAGIC OF A DOG:
BUILT TO COMFORT

What is it about dogs that makes them perfect comfort machines? The combination of their heightened senses and innate physical capabilities make them profoundly effective responders to our moods, health and emotions. Dogs use their whole body to communicate love and comfort to us. We can learn so much from them.

PAWS
Don't underestimate the power of the paws. They work as shock absorbers and brakes. They help the dog navigate slippery or steep slopes and they insulate the inner foot tissues from extreme temperatures.

FUR
Pet and play with a dog, and your brain soon releases the feel-good endorphins serotonin and prolactin. After 15 minutes, your levels of the stress-hormone cortisol decrease significantly.

TAIL

The wag-o-meter is one of best mood indicators out there. We see wagging tails when they're happy and tails between the legs when they feel threatened. Just as humans use smiles and other body language as social cues, our canine friends have their own social cues, including the tail.

BRAIN

The mind of a dog is similar to the mind of a 2-3 year old human. Doesn't that just make perfect sense? Imagine if we could all retain the outlook of life through the innocence of a 2 year old. Full of curiosity, adventure, joy and wonder.

EYES

Dogs are not exactly colorblind. While dogs can't see all colors, studies show dogs can see in various shades of blue and yellows. They can see best at dusk and dawn. Their low-light vision is much better than a human's, but their overall vision is not better.

NOSE

Dogs interpret their world predominantly by smell. The part of a dog's brain that controls smell is 40 times larger than in humans. A dog's sense of smell is up to 100,000 times more accurate than a human's. When dogs smell something they are actually smelling a story. Ever wonder how dogs intuitively sometimes know when a person needs comfort? Recent studies have shown that dogs do indeed rely on their smell to pick up emotions around them.

MOUTH

They certainly use their mouths more for licking than humans do. Maybe because we're too busy talking. Dogs "talk" with their ears, eyes, body posture, fur elevation, tail semaphore and more.

EARS

Dogs have an amazing sense of hearing. Their ability to distinguish who they are with is more based on hearing than sight. They can hear about 4 times the distance of a human. Dogs also have the ability to hear higher pitched sounds not heard by humans.

HEART

In the same manner that young humans show empathy and understanding of the emotions of others, so do dogs.

LESSONS WE LEARN FROM OUR DOGS

There are experts among us that instinctively know how to comfort those who are hurting. Dogs. Watching and learning from them is a great place to start our journey of comfort. Think about how you feel when you're with your pup. And then remember – connecting with humans around you who are struggling can be like that. It doesn't have to be hard. Be like Fido.

THEY RECOGNIZE WHEN YOU'RE HURTING

If you have a dog, you know how they pay attention. They always seem to "know" when you need them. If you're having a bad day they are there at your side. If you're home sick they snuggle with you. They are always looking for ways to love you because that's what makes them happy. As humans, we are not as good at this. We spend most of our time thinking about our own hurts instead of others who are hurting.

THEY PUT YOU FIRST

A dog's main goal is to please others - You are the
only thing on their mind. They aren't on their phones
or too busy for you. They aren't watching TV or
working. They are there for you and happy to see you.
We feel loved and special when someone puts us first.

THEY ARE PRESENT

When they are with you, they are WITH you... They are present - When you have a dog, you know they will be there for you. You know you aren't bothering them. You can tell that there is no place they would rather be and that they love you no matter what. You feel that they understand you when others don't. Even if you messed up. This creates a bond of trust and love. This is connecting with compassion. This is comfort.

THEY LISTEN

They are always just here to love you and listen. They don't talk back. They don't try to give you advice, they just listen. For many of us humans, this is very hard to do. We are busy and listening is slow. We want results fast when comfort is not at all about a quick fix. We watch our love for dogs increase when they let us vent and love us back. We can do the same for each other.

THEY DON'T JUDGE OR HOLD GRUDGES

Sometimes we have a hard time letting go of things that bother us about each other. We make assumptions and judgements and this gets in the way of connecting. We avoid each other, get frustrated and let bad feelings simmer. Dogs don't think this way. They just see someone they love and want to be with. They forgive. Dogs always forgive. They don't hold our mistakes against us. And this makes us love them even more.

THEY DON'T NEED WORDS

Sometimes we just don't know what to say to people when they are struggling. We are afraid to say the wrong thing and make things worse. Many times, we avoid any interaction with that person because of this fear. Then we watch dogs. And it ends up not being so much about the words – but rather, the caring loving hugs, the eye to eye contact and most of all just being together. Comfort does not have to be about what we say.

THEY HELP US GET OUT OF OUR OWN HEADS

In our sadness and brokenness, we can sometimes focus most of our attention on ourselves and our own problems. We overthink things. There is something about a dog that snaps us out of that. Because as much as they take care of us, we feel the urge to take care of them. And that pulls the focus off of ourselves and by helping them, we actually help ourselves.

THEY WANT TO BE WITH US

Dogs don't withdraw when life gets them down. They don't put
headphones on and go through life ignoring other dogs or people.
They are pack animals and so are we. They are happiest when
they are around dogs or people. We are the same. We are wired to
be happiest when we share life together. Our ups and downs our
hurts and our fears. We are not at our best when we are alone.

THEY COMFORT ANYONE & EVERYONE

They comfort those they don't know without any bit of awkward. Have you ever watched a dog go up to a total stranger wagging their tail? And in doing so making that person happy? Us humans don't think that way. We avoid people we don't know even if we know they are hurting. Dogs help fill the gap of loneliness for many people because of this. They love to help. We can do that too.

THEY SHOW UP

Again and again and again for as long as they live. Comfort is not a one and done kind of action. People need comfort every day. Over and over. And when we watch dogs, we see how they blend together comforting and loving and playing. Sometimes within a span of minutes. They intuitively know what is needed at any given time. We can learn from this.

THEY ARE LOYAL

They always assume the best in us. They give us the benefit of the doubt every time. Humans are sometimes afraid to share our feelings with others. It could be that we are afraid that our friends won't keep it to themselves and will share it with others or announce to the world on social media. Dogs don't think that way. No shaming and blaming in their world. They are loyal and confidential. And this makes us love them all the more.

THEY BRING JOY

They don't take life too seriously. They know when to comfort, but they also know when to lighten the mood. They can do something so silly that you can't help but laugh even when you are at your lowest. And for these bits of laughter, we love them even more and love to have them around. You can bring joy too.

THEY ARE UNITERS – NOT DIVIDERS

The are inclusive not exclusive. There is no such thing as a "clique" with dogs. They bring people together. They allow us to focus on what unites us instead of what divides us apart. They choose love first above anything else. And in today's divisive and critical society, this is something we can all learn from.

THEY ARE GENUINE

They always reflect who they are and aren't worried about what people think. They don't photoshop images on an instagram page. They don't hide their feelings and they don't compare themselves with others. When they want to play, we know it. When they are hungry, we know it. And when they just want attention, we know that too. And we love them for it.

DIVERSITY NEVER GETS IN THEIR WAY

Dogs are incredibly diverse. More than 400 breeds. And they don't let any characteristics of their breed get in their way of connecting with others and loving them. There simply is no delineation along the lines of fur color or fur length or floppy ears or pointy ears or long tails or short tails or tall or short. Go to a dog park if you want to watch this in action.

THEY PAWS

They slow down when they need to and never get too busy. They instinctively know how to manage their time and take care of their whole body so they can take care of others. "Pawsing" to see, to do, to love, to play and to rest. The key to comforting others. You can do this too.

THEY PLAY

Playing is fun for sure. We have as much fun playing with our dogs as they have fun playing with us. But playing serves a more important purpose for dogs. It keeps them physically and mentally strong. We need that too.

THEY DO THIS EVERY DAY

It's who they are. It's who we should be. They will wake up and do it all again tomorrow. They spend their lives focused on others. Each moment of each day, they want to be with others and make them happy. It's their DNA. It's also in our DNA, but most of us have allowed personal fears and troubles to suppress our innate ability to comfort.

SEARCHING FOR A SOLUTION: DOGS AS OUR TEACHERS

I remember the day I knew we needed to do more like it was yesterday.

It started with a phone call. As I saw the name pop up, I already dreaded hearing what I was about to hear on the other end of the line. It was the Principal of a school, in tears. *"There's been a horrible accident..."*

By the time the call was over, I had learned of the death of a student– and the impending shattering of an entire student body and community. Knowing a crushing truth before others and just waiting to watch it unfold is a a horrible feeling.

Once again, it was my job to show up with LCC K-9 Comfort Dogs and to bring love and comfort to those whose lives were about to change forever.

At one point on this particular deployment, I found myself sitting in a circle with the best friends of the brother of the student who died. They were leaning on each other and leaning on the dogs. They were talking about their friend and feeling helpless. One by one, those students sitting in the circle all admitted the same thing. Not one of them had reached out to the brother yet. Not one. The conversations went something like this: "I can't even imagine how he's going to come back to school." "Have you talked to him yet?" No, I haven't". "Me neither." Silence. And just put a quick mental image in your head of what it must have been like for that friend of theirs at that moment. Home in an empty house, separated from his normal world and staring at his phone with no notifications popping up.

These students had not yet reached out, not because they didn't *want* to, but because they didn't know how. They were afraid they would say the wrong thing. They were afraid that they would make it worse. They thought that the family might want to be together and not be bothered. They didn't want to do something different than their friends were doing.

So the brother, grieving at home, was left wondering why no one cared to reach out.

What these kids are experiencing is the Awkward Zone™. They are used to happy Instagrams, funny snaps, shared photos of sporting events, concerts and talk of college. No one has adequately prepared them for being the broken one. Or comforting the broken one.

In this case, like many crisis responses, I was there to support the students for three days. Then it's "back to normal". School administrators feel pressured to "move on" while the empty chair still sits in the classroom and the world of many students has become unrecognizable.

Between these short-term deployments and the weekly visits to Sandy Hook Elementary I started to feel a need to do more. All I could think of was the old adage "If you give a man a fish, he will eat for a day. If you teach a man to fish, he will eat for a lifetime." I saw comparisons in that phrase to what I was doing. I loved bringing comfort to those who were hurting. But as the weeks, months and years started passing. I couldn't help thinking– now what?

I found myself asking the same questions over and over again.:

"What happens to these shattered lives when the comfort or therapy dogs leave?"

"What is it about dogs and why are they so needed?"

"What has changed? We didn't have support dogs when I grew up."

"What is it that dogs do that we don't do ourselves?"

"How can we stay connected to those who are isolated and hurting?"

"Can we move from only "giving" comfort to actually "equipping" comfort?"

"Can we teach humans to be more like dogs?"

In my head, again and again was this phrase–encouraging me to take it on:

"You can give a person comfort and they will be comforted for a day. If you teach them how to comfort, they will feel the power of comfort for a lifetime."

Could it work?

And so that's what led to Inspiring Comfort, LLC and this book. I felt in the depths of my soul that we have to do more.

We need to be more like dogs. We need to relearn the skill of comforting.

> No one had adequately prepared them for being the broken one –or comforting the broken one.

"Caring for others tends to be the first cut when we review our personal time budget. It does not necessarily fulfill the goals of my ambition; it will not pave the way for my success; it takes away from my own depleted emotional resources. It is an imposition in every way. To some of us, it is an inconvenience from which we unashamedly run. We have become experts in maintaining a grand scope of friendships and amateurs in genuine intimacy and care. Unwittingly, we have sacrificed everything on the altar of self-sufficiency - only to discover that we have sold our souls to isolation."

– Sandy Oshiro Rosen

PART TWO

THE CASE FOR COMFORT

We've all been there

The evolution of comfort

Where we are today

When we don't comfort:
The price we pay in the
workplace

WHY WE DON'T COMFORT:
WE'VE ALL BEEN THERE

What happens when we are caught off guard and don't know what to do?

THE SUPERMARKET

The scene takes place every day in supermarkets across America. On one end of the store someone walks in who wishes more than anything they didn't have to be out in public, but they must eat. In this case her name is Jane. She unexpectedly lost her husband and doesn't want to talk to anyone. Jane is hoping to get through the store without running into people she knows. She's hurting, grieving, lonely, traumatized and depressed.

On the other end of the store enters Suzie. She's in a hurry and has exactly 8 minutes to get the 10 things on her list before picking up her son from soccer. Jane and Suzie know each other but it's been awhile since they've spoken. Somewhere mid store they turn the corner and find themselves in the same aisle.

Enter the Awkward Zone™.

Suzie is frozen. She knows what Jane is going through, but they have not spoken. On top of that she has neglected to do anything. She didn't attend the wake or funeral, hasn't called, sent a card, or an email, a casserole, or a text. She maybe hit the sad face emoji on a Facebook posting but didn't even comment. That's been it. So, she is stuck. Caught between

not knowing what to say and wanting to walk fast to the next aisle. Many people would move to the next aisle to avoid the encounter, but Suzie is a talker so she decides to talk to Jane

Both Jane and Suzie dread this moment. For Jane, she wants to be seen and loved but she also knows that the odds are that Suzie will be awkward and say something that ends up being anything but helpful. For Suzie, because she's not prepared for this moment, she will be awkward and will say things without much thought. Her intentions are good - she really does want to help Jane - but she is just not trained and equipped to know what to do. So, the awkwardness takes over .... "Oh Jane! I'm so sorry for your loss. How are you?" asks Suzie. Jane replies "I'm doing ok, thanks", and Suzie finishes up with "please let me know if you need anything." "Ok, thanks" replies Jane. End of awkward conversation.

Jane of course will never get back to Suzie with things she needs help with, she can't even remember what day of the week it is. Suzie walks away wondering if she said the wrong thing. The encounter leaves both Jane and Suzie feeling worse.

THE WORKPLACE
The scene takes place every day in workplaces across America.

Keith, a member of

We often walk away wondering if we said the wrong thing.

your team left in a hurry after he got word of a crisis. Your initial instinct is to feel bad for him. You send him a text to see if he is ok. But you are also worried that the work won't get done. (he's actually worried that the work won't get done as well). Keith takes some time off as you scramble to delegate out the work and get everything done.

The office manager sent flowers and a few coworkers made calls, but when it's time for Keith to come back to work, he walks straight back into the awkward zone.

Keith walks into work vowing to get "back to normal" and will fake being ok. Some employees feel resentment as they have had to pick up some of the slack and don't understand why he had to take so much time off work. Other employees desperately want to do something for him but are afraid to say anything for fear of "making it worse". This is a "workplace" after all, we aren't supposed to look weak and talk too much about personal issues. We are there to get a job done, right? Although more than half of our day is often spent with our co-workers, true connections of care and support are rare. As the days and weeks pass of Keith faking it, everyone just assumes he's "moved on."

In reality, this department has now moved further apart in its team bond and unity because of the lack of open communication, expression of emotions and one-to-one connectedness. The elephant in the room sits in the way of everything. Furthermore, because of this unaddressed issue, this team will now have a more difficult time working together effectively because some unresolved issues are hanging in the air. People feel the shift in team spirit. Productivity will suffer. Keith will forever feel misunderstood by his colleagues during his darkest days.

It doesn't have to be this way.

THE COFFEE SHOP
It happens every day in coffee shops across America.

You're sitting with a group of friends talking about your plans for the weekend. You look up and see someone from your history class walk in. She's not really part of your friend group, in fact the friends you're with don't know her. But you've worked on a project together and have hung out with her a few times and like her. And from your Instagram, you are aware of her anger at her parents recent divorce. She comes in to grab her mobile order looking like she's crying with her head down.

> You think about the fact that she could start crying and not want to talk.

Enter the Awkward Zone. Your heart pulls at you to go and say hi. It hurts you to see her sad. If you get up to go to her, it would require you to break away from your group and explain to them how you know her. You might feel that you should invite her to join, but you don't feel like it's the right time and place for that. And with seeing her upset, you are afraid to approach her. It's a crowded place and you don't want to do anything to make it more awkward. You think about the fact that she could start crying and not want to talk. Or say "Leave me alone" and walk out leaving you standing there.

You end up doing nothing and as you watch her leave, you feel bad that you didn't act. On her end, she leaves the shop feeling even worse. She saw people she knew having fun and no one even approached her. She felt alone coming into the coffee shop and leaves feeling more alone leaving because no one cared.

It doesn't have to be this way.

When we open our eyes to the circumstances around us and when we better understand what needs to be done, we don't have to enter the awkward zone in the supermarket, in the workplace, in a coffee shop, in our schools & communities... anywhere.

LOOKING BACK TO MOVE FORWARD:
THE EVOLUTION OF COMFORT

No matter how long you have traveled in the wrong direction you always have the choice to turn around.
–Heather K. Jones

Responding to tragic situations was so different when I was growing up in rural Wisconsin in the 60's and 70's. Like it is today, the comforting process would usually start with communication thru a phone, but this time the phone was attached to the wall and had a human at the other end, not a hastily texted message. Once the call was over, it was humans who swung into action and not comfort/therapy dogs or sad face emojis. The ladies would make some casseroles and jello, and us kids would hold those dishes on our laps in the car as we headed over to whoever was enduring the crisis. I don't recall there being an awkwardness. We just went and most times hung out at the house and

helped with whatever needed to be done. As a child without a phone in hand, I had to find a way to occupy myself, sometimes called to help with dishes, taking out the trash or any other odd job that I could do.

When I was about 10, an acquaintance of my parents was tragically killed. I didn't really know this family at the time, but soon was very familiar with the family, their friends and their house, as my mom would frequently help with errands and bring food. Over the years, I would listen to my parents phone calls with Ellen, the surviving widow, as she took over the family business and navigated through life. I got to know them better and better, and still today Ellen is a dear friend who

I stay in touch with. I know in my heart that I would have never known Ellen and her family the way I do today if I wasn't at my moms side as she and my dad cared for her and her family over the years.

But what I also remember about my childhood was the broader community of comfort that kicked in. We were not at all the only family helping out. It was a community effort. Usually organized through the church where everyone saw each other every week. I was taught to give hugs and send cards. To show love and compassion for all of those who were hurting. It's just what we did. It was remembering anniversaries and birthdays of those who had passed, and it was bringing over fruit baskets during the holidays knowing they would be going through a rough time.

What has changed since then?

"It wasn't all that long ago that it was standard in our culture for people to officially be in mourning for a full year. They wore black. They didn't go to parties. They didn't smile a whole lot. And everybody accepted their period of mourning; no one ridiculed a mother in black or asked her stupid questions about why she was still so sad. Obviously, this is no longer accepted practice; mourners are encouraged to quickly move on, turn the corner, get back to work, think of the positive, be grateful for what is left, have another baby, and other unkind, unfeeling, obtuse and downright cruel comments. What does this say about us – other than we're terribly uncomfortable with death, with grief, with mourning, with loss – or we're so self absorbed that we easily forget the profound suffering the loss of a child created in the shattered parents and remaining children."

—KAY WARREN, FACEBOOK POST

CREATING A TIMELINE OF COMFORT

Over these past almost seven years of supporting those who need comfort, one thing has become extremely clear. Times are changing fast and most things today are not as they used to be, including how we care for each other. We have seen this play out in our programs and workshops, so we set out to capture what's behind these changes.

We started by researching specific areas of where and how we have traditionally cared for and comforted each other. From there we created timelines of well documented historical events and studies in each of these areas to visualize just how quickly things have changed and continue to change.

When we consider that these changes are happening in a relatively short amount of time in human history, we can better grasp why so many of us are feeling the not so subtle shifts of loneliness, isolation, anxiety and depression. Human behaviors of care were relatively unchanged from the beginning of recorded history until well into the 1900's. Each area where we have historically cared for, supported and comforted each other has been flipped on its head the past 7-8 decades. The last two decades have been especially profound.

As we recapped the information, an intern on the team, Byron, made the following observation: "Everything I looked at - everything - has shifted away from being there for each other. We are distancing ourselves from everyone and everything. There is a great shift going on, most linked to advancements in technology. What is astounding to me is how quickly everything is changing."

It's impossible to look at the last column of the chart from the year 2000 forward and not wonder how such massive trends are interrelating to each other. Is it a coincidence that the mental health epidemic emerges in the middle of all of these other shifts?

There are real reasons why it's becoming awkward and more difficult to reach out to those who need it. So let's understand these trends in order to move forward and find our own unique approaches to caring for those who desperately need us.

> "Everything I looked at - *everything* - has shifted away from being there for each other."
> -BYRON BUSHARA

PRIOR TO 1900

1900-1950

HOW WE COMMUNICATE

Communication is all face to face verbal or hand written. Only with the new inventions such as the first telephone in 1876 did verbal communications across distance begin.

While communication is still mostly face to face verbal and hand written, telephones are installed in businesses and homes at a rapid pace. Phone booths and pay phones become available for those on the go.

HOW WE GRIEVE

Families are responsible for burials. Recognized period of mourning

Funeral homes run by undertakers start to spring up across the United States. Mass atrocities caused during the World Wars start to desensitize an entire population to the grieving process.

HOW WE CARE FOR THE AGING

We take care of the elderly within our family homes, and are supported by community efforts. Elderly without families or communities are left to poorhouses.

Poorhouses decline. The Social Security Act is introduced in 1935, providing federal support and benefits for the elderly.

HOW WE MEDICALLY CARE FOR OURSELVES AND OTHERS

A local doctor or famiilies are the main souce of healthcare. Some places have no doctor at all.

Advancements in medicine start to occur around the turn of the century. New medications to treat illnesses and to alleviate pain begin to be developed. Access to hospitals greatly expand.

HOW WE FORM SOCIAL CONNECTIONS

People socialize within their family, closest neighbors, and houses of worship.

While families, neighbors, and religious establishments are still the main forms of socializing, schools and workplaces begin to enter the scene for social engagement.

0		1000 AD		1900 AD	TODAY 2020

MODERN PERIOD OF RAPID CHANGE

1950-2000

2000-PRESENT

Face to face verbal and hand written communication is heavily assisted by technological advances. The following emerge at a rapid pace: dial phones, touch-tone phones, pagers, fax machines, 5 lb mobile phones, flip phones, desk top computers, world wide web, and emails.

A shift away from face-to-face, one-to-one communication as hand-held computers, smart phones, and social media emerge at a rapid pace.

With the advent of television, cable news, violent movies and video games; violence, dying, and dealth become common place in all forms of our news and entertainment.

Non- stop access to coverage of mass tragedies on social media has further desensitized a population to not know how to support those that are grieving. Because we "move on" to constantly updated news, there is a "move on" mentality to human pain, struggles and grief.

Nursing homes, hospices and assisted living care come on to the scene providing support for the elderly outside of our homes.

It is less common for families to care for the elderly in their homes, as elder care resources and facilities are the norm.

Life expancy grows as advancements in medical care rise. The field of Mental Health emerges with new drugs being introduced for the first time for depression.

Changes in health care regulations, provider networks and insurance coverage increase the burden for indiviuals to manage their care. The Mental Health Epidemic emerges.

Easy air travel begins to split more families. Dual-income and single-parent homes and families rise. Globalization becomes a buzz word. As the pace and stress of life increases, the workplace and schools grow in where we socialize.

As social connections move online, families split farther apart and religious affiliation continues decline, the workplace, schools, and hobbies emerge as this era's main face-to-face social centers.

HOW WE COMMUNICATE

Over the last century, communication has quickly moved from all face to face and hand written to mostly digitally assisted communication. Methods of person to person interaction through technology and social media are developing at a rapid pace - faster than we are able to learn how to adjust and balance. As a result, intimate face-to-face interaction has become less common and more awkward.

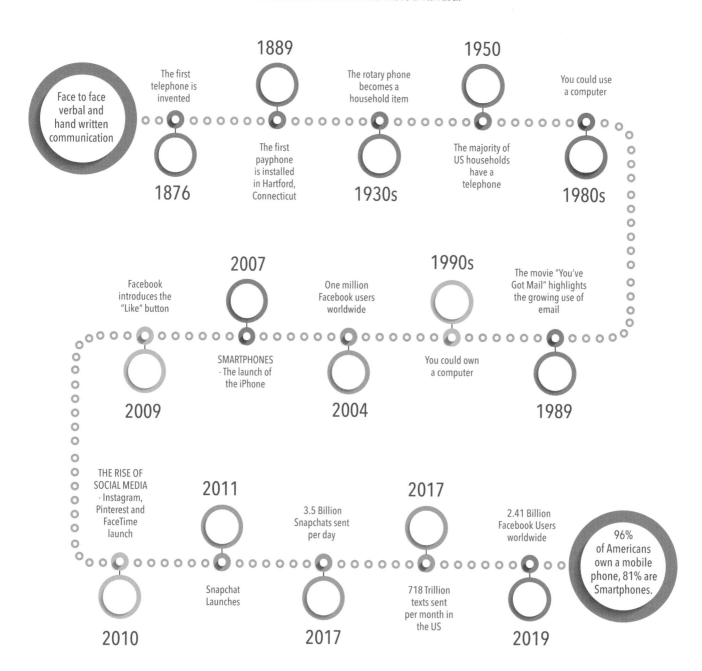

Face to face verbal and hand written communication

1876
The first telephone is invented

1889
The first payphone is installed in Hartford, Connecticut

1930s
The rotary phone becomes a household item

1950
The majority of US households have a telephone

1980s
You could use a computer

1989
The movie "You've Got Mail" highlights the growing use of email

1990s
You could own a computer

2004
One million Facebook users worldwide

2007
SMARTPHONES - The launch of the iPhone

2009
Facebook introduces the "Like" button

2010
THE RISE OF SOCIAL MEDIA - Instagram, Pinterest and FaceTime launch

2011
Snapchat Launches

2017
3.5 Billion Snapchats sent per day

2017
718 Trillion texts sent per month in the US

2019
2.41 Billion Facebook Users worldwide

96% of Americans own a mobile phone, 81% are Smartphones.

HOW WE GRIEVE

Mourning and grieving has transformed over the last century; we have moved from smaller and more intimate support and being there long term, to public funerals and tragic news spreading quickly on social media. In addition, with an increase of non-stop coverage of mass tragedies, we have become desensitized to violence and death, now accepting it as a weekly event. This quick news cycle changes the way our attention stays on any given event and we can easily forget just how long term pain and suffering can be. All of this has lead to front-loaded support as soon as a tragedy happens, and very little long term support for those who are suffering.

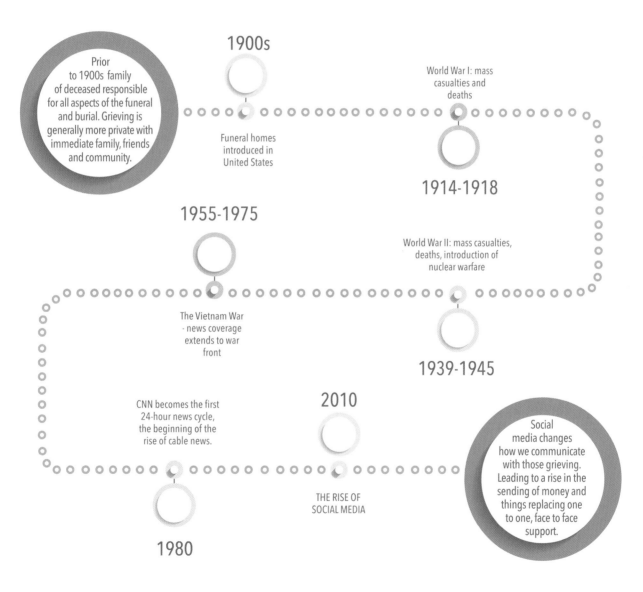

Prior to 1900s family of deceased responsible for all aspects of the funeral and burial. Grieving is generally more private with immediate family, friends and community.

1900s

Funeral homes introduced in United States

World War I: mass casualties and deaths

1914-1918

1955-1975

World War II: mass casualties, deaths, introduction of nuclear warfare

The Vietnam War - news coverage extends to war front

1939-1945

CNN becomes the first 24-hour news cycle, the beginning of the rise of cable news.

2010

Social media changes how we communicate with those grieving. Leading to a rise in the sending of money and things replacing one to one, face to face support.

THE RISE OF SOCIAL MEDIA

1980

HOW WE CARE FOR THE AGING

This last century has seen a large shift in the way we care for our seniors - from family centered care to professional centered care. The later part of the 20th century saw an explosion in nursing home facilities, assisted living centers and memory care centers. At the same time, our history's lowest levels of multigenerational living arrangements. For those who do stay with their families, the caregivers are so exhausted there is sometimes little time left for meaningful conversation. Underlying this, diminished vision, hearing and memory make can make interactions difficult. The loneliness epidemic is hitting seniors and their caregivers extremely hard.

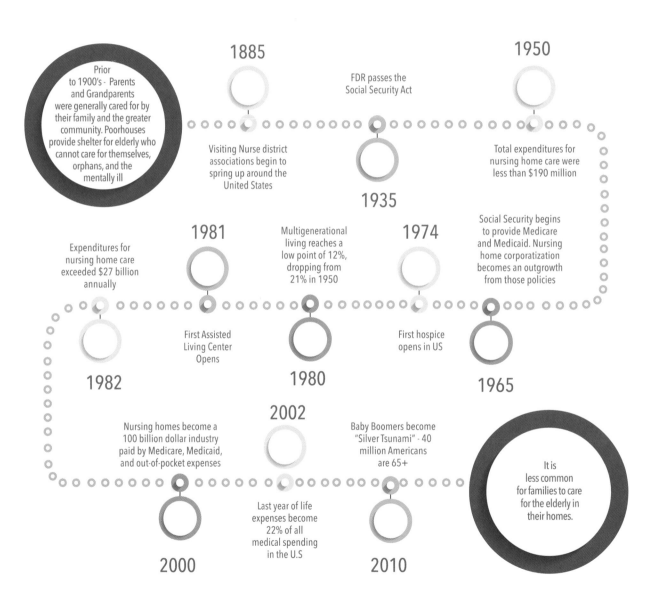

Prior to 1900's - Parents and Grandparents were generally cared for by their family and the greater community. Poorhouses provide shelter for elderly who cannot care for themselves, orphans, and the mentally ill

1885
Visiting Nurse district associations begin to spring up around the United States

FDR passes the Social Security Act

1935

1950
Total expenditures for nursing home care were less than $190 million

Social Security begins to provide Medicare and Medicaid. Nursing home corporatization becomes an outgrowth from those policies

Expenditures for nursing home care exceeded $27 billion annually

1981
First Assisted Living Center Opens

Multigenerational living reaches a low point of 12%, dropping from 21% in 1950

1974
First hospice opens in US

1982

1980

1965

2002
Last year of life expenses become 22% of all medical spending in the U.S

Baby Boomers become "Silver Tsunami" - 40 million Americans are 65+

It is less common for families to care for the elderly in their homes.

Nursing homes become a 100 billion dollar industry paid by Medicare, Medicaid, and out-of-pocket expenses

2000

2010

HOW WE MEDICALLY CARE
FOR OURSELVES AND OTHERS

People are living longer but not necessarily more healthy lives this century. Advances in all areas of medicine are allowing those with severe illness and injury to live, where a century ago they would not have.

In addition, the number of years that people live with chronic diseases and disabilities, like depression, back pain, arthritis and diabetes, has also increased.

Another critical area that more fully developed this last century is the field of Mental Health. The recognition that the care of our minds is as important as the care of our bodies is a relatively new concept. An explosion in mental health diagnosis, medications and mental health support structures have been layered into our health care system.

Underlying all of this, rising medical costs bring financial stress with 66% of adults citing the cost of health insurance as a stressor, while 63% cite uncertainly about the future both of their own health and that of others as a source of stress.

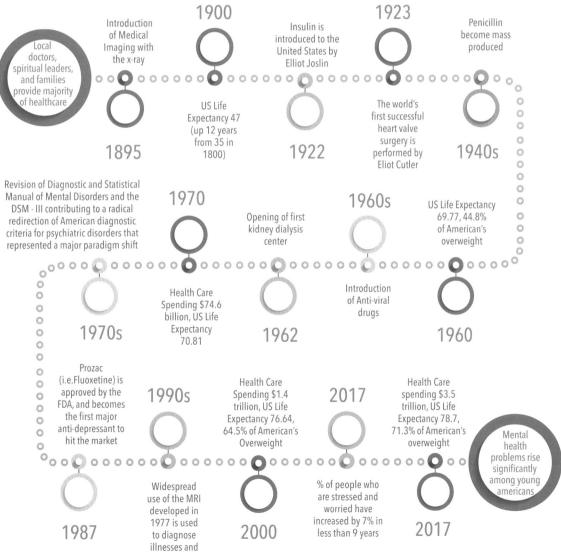

HOW WE FORM SOCIAL CONNECTIONS

Throughout most of human history bonds between parents, children, relatives and the village community drove social interaction. During the 20th century the main hubs of our social connections rapidly began to shift. The community of the front porch gave way to the TV. With access to air and ground travel, families moved farther away from each other to pursue their best jobs or preferred climate. Religious affiliation is on the decline and online communities have grown dramatically. As centuries old family and community bonds weaken, online forums, schools and workplaces are now being leaned on to fill that social connection gap. As these traditional forms of connections have weakened, so have our human care skills.

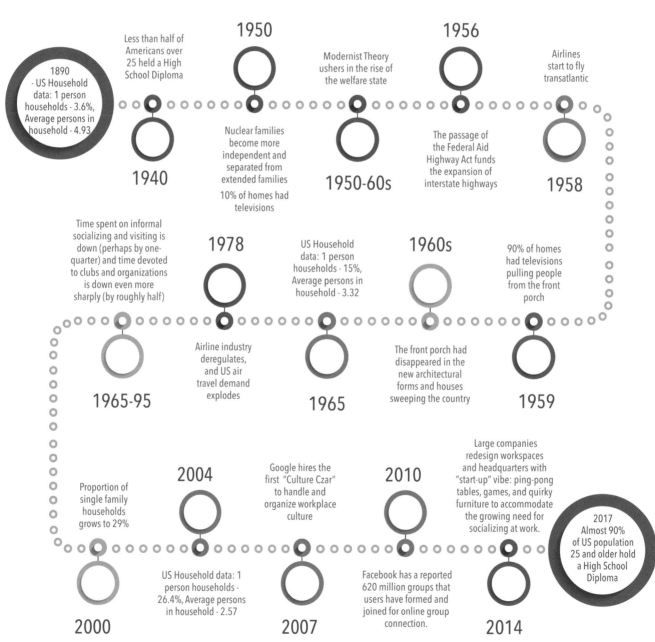

1890 - US Household data: 1 person households - 3.6%, Average persons in household - 4.93.

Less than half of Americans over 25 held a High School Diploma

1940

1950

Nuclear families become more independent and separated from extended families

10% of homes had televisions

Modernist Theory ushers in the rise of the welfare state

1950-60s

1956

The passage of the Federal Aid Highway Act funds the expansion of interstate highways

Airlines start to fly transatlantic

1958

Time spent on informal socializing and visiting is down (perhaps by one-quarter) and time devoted to clubs and organizations is down even more sharply (by roughly half)

1978

Airline industry deregulates, and US air travel demand explodes

1965-95

US Household data: 1 person households - 15%, Average persons in household - 3.32

1965

1960s

The front porch had disappeared in the new architectural forms and houses sweeping the country

90% of homes had televisions pulling people from the front porch

1959

Proportion of single family households grows to 29%

2004

Google hires the first "Culture Czar" to handle and organize workplace culture

2010

Large companies redesign workspaces and headquarters with "start-up" vibe: ping-pong tables, games, and quirky furniture to accommodate the growing need for socializing at work.

2017 Almost 90% of US population 25 and older hold a High School Diploma

US Household data: 1 person households - 26.4%, Average persons in household - 2.57

2000

2007

Facebook has a reported 620 million groups that users have formed and joined for online group connection.

2014

When A Barn Burned

A look back on how we used to care for each other.

by Betty Reul

I grew up in wonderful rural Iowa in the 1940's and 50's. My parents owned a garage and filling station which, together with a small grocery store/pub and the local creamery (where farmers brought their milk to be made into butter), was the hub of a farming community.

Family lived near and neighbors were as important in our lives as family. We celebrated together, we worshipped together, and we shared joy and sadness together. There were many occasions to be together: birthdays, weddings, funerals, or just to have a good time!

Probably nothing brought the community together more than a disaster: tornado, fire, illness or death. Barn fires were among the most devastating. At those times,

the community really rallied. There was an urgency, not only was the family affected in distress but their source of income was disrupted.

Because of the close relationships of the local people, getting help to those in need happened quite automatically. As soon as the news of the disaster was shared, usually through the local telephone switchboard, helping with the restoration was top priority.

Some would tend to the livestock and house them until the barn was rebuilt, some would handle the razing and clean-up, while others offered needed support and comfort to the family. A new barn was built with the labor of the neighborhood. Everyone would prepare and bring food to

the family and for those doing the physical work. It was the total focus of the community.

Having grown up in that environment, I find it concerning to see just how much our society has deviated from that today. Our dependence on each other has diminished. Younger generations have moved away from their home communities, neighbors are no longer critical for our well-being, there's little time to entertain guests in our homes.

Each of the steps of progress has enabled us to be more independent and less dependent on others. But it has me wondering, at what cost? People's social and emotional needs are still the same. We still need to be there for each other.

WHERE WE ARE TODAY: OUR CURRENT REALITY

Stores and statistics from the frontline that underscore the case for relearning the skill of comfort

PERSPECTIVES FROM A TEACHER

Our students today live in a world of constant media influence. I teach students that look at the perfect world created in magazines, television shows, and social media. I teach early elementary students that are dressed like fashion models and sneak makeup to school. I teach students who think reality television is real. I teach students who smile on the outside but have immense internal sadness. I teach students ostracized by their friends on social media. I teach students of all ages that are considering suicide, seeing it as their only option to end loneliness or bullying. I teach students scarred by the trauma they have seen or experienced firsthand. I teach students who do not know how to communicate with each other. I teach students who do self-harm. I teach students who appear to not care about anything

Julie Wall teaches art to students age 4 to 60+.

"I teach students who do not know how to communicate with each other."

JULIE WALL,
TEACHER

DANIEL MATTILA
LCSW

"I believe that we can make a significant impact by intentionally connecting and providing constructive, real-life companionship."

"We have so much work to do and it all starts with comfort."

LAURA MAYER
DIRECTOR, CRISIS LINK

PSYCHOTHERAPIST VIEW

For over 20 years, I have been a psychotherapist in private practice. I have seen the rise of a significant problem that continues to worsen. That problem is disconnection, loneliness, and social isolation. In the past two decades, technology and social media have drastically changed the ways that people communicate and connect. Human relationships, whether they are friendships, intimate relationships, or affiliations with groups, have become cyber relationships. While this can have positive effects, it can also become very isolating.

Human beings crave touch and real-life companionship. Studies show how brain chemistry is positively affected by physical touch with another living being. As human beings, we are programmed to be in relationships. I believe that we can make a significant impact by intentionally connecting and providing constructive, real-life companionship. This kind of companionship is soothing, healing, and therapeutic. Not only that, however. This kind of connection also helps us to be better humans by fostering love, compassion, and empathy.

Daniel E. Mattila, M.Div., LCSW in Private Practice

CRISIS LINE DIRECTOR

Our understanding of why people suffer, and the underlying causes of suffering has grown dramatically. Despite all this growth in knowledge one thing remains the same: connection and empathy are critical aspects of the human experience and without them people suffer. As the Director of a 24/7 crisis center, I see firsthand the power of caring. In the 50 years since our crisis hotline started, the need has never declined and has grown exponentially.

Over time pop culture has placed an emphasis on self-care and activities that people do alone. They try deep breathing, yoga and long walks. For some, these coping skills are helpful, but what most people want is a caring human to be with them in their despair. Breathing apps, coloring books, and walking can only provide so much comfort. People land in our crisis center hurting, alone and in need of caring others. People do not call crisis hotlines because they need advice, they call because they need human care and connection. If we are to get serious about addressing the underlying pain that leads to so many challenges in people's lives, we must go back to the human foundation which is caring and comforting one another. We have so much work to do and it all starts with comfort.

Laura Mayer - Director, PRS CrisisLink, Washington DC

"They call because they need human care and connection".

WHY WE NEED COMFORT *NOW*

72
THOUSAND

Annual drug related deaths in the US, three times what it was in 2000

18%

Adults in the United States that suffer from mental illness of some kind

89
BILLION

Amount spent annually on mental illness in the US

DEPRESSION ALONE IS ESTIMATED TO COST THE AMERICAN ECONOMY $210 BILLION ANNUALLY.

–KESSLER, R. C.

The Costs of Depression (2012)
Psychiatric Clinics of North America

31%

Increase in deaths by suicide from 2000-2015 of adults in the United States

1/2

American adults who report always or sometimes feeling lonely

30
MILLION

Adults in the US suffering from anxiety (9% of the population)

PRESIDENT OF A MILLENIAL DRIVEN WORKFORCE

"Banana gate" was just the beginning. Then, Summer Fridays. Followed by the pet policy. These kinds of decisions were my new normal as the leader of a company that is proudly for young people and by young people. I had just turned 50, had spent the first 25+ years of my career in a corporate environment, and had been the youngest among my work colleagues at established technology and financial services firms. But, a chance meeting and unexpected connections brought me to a company in hyper-growth mode, brimming with eager, talented and ambitious young people. They cared deeply about the business we were building and passionately about the culture we were collectively nurturing. That meant they wanted ripe bananas on Mondays and to "work from anywhere" on Fridays. Their dogs should be allowed in the office and it would be great to get a discount on pet insurance. Flexible hours are a rule not an exception and please keep cold brew on tap, even in the winter.

At first, I was amazed, then annoyed by the audacity of the expectations. In the gray walled, cubicle-maze offices I grew up in we personally funded the monthly "coffee club" and we brought in "World's Best Mom" mugs from home because our office didn't provide paper cups, let alone fresh fruit. On Fridays, all year long, we worked, at the office, while our dogs stayed home. This was the workplace as I knew it and the corporate norms that had been established for decades. And, now leading a team of millennial and generation Z employees, I realized just how much is changing. This class of office professionals is rewriting the rules in a way that I believe is more humane and creates a seamless flow between work and, well, just living. They're creating cultures designed to help people love what they do and where they do it. The role of the workplace has shifted. It's not just where work happens; it's now also a social hub where valued and valuable relationships are formed.

The role of the workplace has shifted. It's not just where work happens; it's now also a social hub where valued and valuable relationships are formed.

By letting well behaved dogs roam our office halls, we're bringing a sense of home and comfort to the often frenetic pace of the work. By offering a simple breakfast (cinnamon toast is an office staple and, yes, a steady supply of bananas), our office kitchen tends to be the place where colleagues become friends. By providing comprehensive wellness benefits that not only include discounts at trendy fitness studios but also mental health therapy sessions, we're helping employees take care of their whole selves. And, by encouraging "work from anywhere" Fridays, we're offering ways for our people to live more balanced, fulfilling lives.

So, let's roll out the yoga mats and raise a glass of cold brew to our new and improved workplaces. This is Work 2.0. And, this generation sees the changes that need to happen and are doing it right.

Christa Carone is the President of Group Nine Media

THOUGHTS FROM A COLLEGE STUDENT

An Open Letter To My Mental Health

Dear Mental Health,

Hi, it's me Byron. I don't know if you remember me. It's been a couple of years since we've spoken. I guess more like six. It's been rough, I'm not going to lie. It's been pretty rough. Lots of ups and downs, sort of like points undulating across a line. Sometimes I'm really happy, and I'm at the top of the world. And sometimes I'm really down, and I don't feel like going on. The truth is, though, that a lot of the time is spent in between those two extremes. I call that area the grey area. I know I'm definitely not the first person to coin that term. I've heard tons of my friends speak about the grey areas in their relationships. But I think mine is different, because, you see, I call mine the grey area because its void of color.

Sometimes I'm really happy, and I'm at the top of the world. And sometimes I'm really down, and I don't feel like going on.

It sort of feels like I've been shoved into purgatory. It's just grey. That was it. Things didn't make me laugh but they also didn't make me cry. I became numb to the things around me. I no longer hated but I also no longer loved. I became indifferent to the activities I was engaging in. Simply put, I felt nothing. And people say that i'm obviously feeling something, but I have to disagree. Because if I was feeling something, even everything at once, then a visible emotion would come to mind. But I was devoid of emotion.

The funny thing is that sometimes I miss the highs and lows. I know it sounds crazy, but at least in those moments I really felt something. During my highs, I could crack a million jokes a minute and could talk about anything with anyone. During my lows, I could cry to the sad songs I kept handy and write tragic stories about depression. But while I exist, suspended in the grey area, I can't feel anything. No matter how hard I try to laugh at a comedy special I've laughed at a hundred times before, I can't find it within me to find any of the jokes funny. And alternatively, no matter how hard I try and cry to my sad songs, not a single tear is shed. Stabilizing at this dysthymic baseline was sort of like falling in love. Falling in love is fast, like your falling towards earth and gravity is pulling you, and then, all of a sudden, it stops. You reach your maximum velocity, and that becomes normal to you. And so you're no longer falling, not really. You're just suspended. That's how I feel. Suspended. And when you're suspended, well there's really no where else you can go but here. And unless a force pushes you, that's just where you stay. And I guess I'm afraid that this is where I'll stay forever.

Yours, Byron

Byron is a History Major at the College of William & Mary

THE NUMBERS
BEHIND THE NEED:
WHY COMFORT CAN'T
WAIT ANY LONGER

Death by suicide for kids age 10-14 has increased 86% over the past decade

And in particular, there's been a very large increase in the rate among younger kids in the 10 to 14 range, where the rate has increased by 190% in that 10-year period (2000-2017)

Lonely people are more than twice as likely to develop Alzheimer's

Researchers at the Rush Alzheimer's Disease Center in Chicago found that people who are persistently lonely may be more vulnerable to the negative effects of age-related neuropathology.

Loneliness among those over 60 has increased significantly

57% of those age 60 and older are lonely, according to a study from the University of Georgia, which found a 4% increase from 2008 - 2012 alone.

College students visiting counseling centers on campus up by 30%

A study by The Center for Collegiate Mental Health found that from 2009 – 2015, student visits counseling centers on college campuses increased by about 30% on average.

SOURCES: US NEWS AND WORLD REPORT, RUSH MEDICAL CENTER, UNIVERSITY OF GEORGIA, THE CENTER FOR COLLEGIATE MENTAL HEALTH, PENN STATE UNIVERSITY, BRIGHAM YOUNG UNIVERSITY, STUDY FINDS, THE CONVERSATION, IPSOS SURVEY

Major depression increased among teenagers by 52% from 2009-2017

Several studies show increased rates of depression in our teenagers over the last 10 years

Smaller family networks expected to increase by 50% by 2060

Kinless adults (defined as living without a spouse, biological child, parent or sibling) are increasing among people over 50, and may double by 2060 which may result in smaller family networks.

Loneliness can be a bigger health risk than obesity or smoking

A Brigham Young University review of scientific literature found that social isolation increases your risk of death by an astounding 30%, and some estimates have it as high as 60%!

7 out of 10 young adults prefer to communicate digitally than in person

Millennials and the younger Gen Z prefer to communicate digitally – mostly by text message – than in person. 62 percent would rather forget their wallet at home than their phone when going out according to a 2017 LivePerson survey.

Online habits of teens linked to increased suicide risk factors

Teens who spent five or more hours a day online were 71 percent more likely than those who spent less than an hour a day to have at least one suicide risk factor (depression, thinking about suicide, making a suicide plan or attempting suicide).

54% of Americans report feeling as though no one knows them well

Respondents of a 2018 Ipsos survey of 20,000 adults reported they felt left out (47%), their relationships were not meaningful (43%), felt isolated from others (43%), and/or that they are no longer close to anyone (39%).

WHERE WE ARE TODAY: COMFORT IS NOT A CLICK AWAY

"65,000 stuffed animals were sent to a town of 27,000. There were nine tractor-trailers full of paper snowflakes, and a half a million letters".

The media response was fast and chaotic. So many of us remember where we were when we learned of the horrific tragedy at Sandy Hook Elementary. Consider for a moment how we learned of what was happening. Minute by minute, information was shared as events unfolded. Gone are the days when the families of those most impacted in a tragedy are given space to control how to share their loss. On this day, reporters scurried to uncover the next bit of information and got many things wrong. A community was not even able to grasp what was happening while the rest of the world was glued to their screens awaiting each new update. Everyone learning information - whether true or false - at the same time.

Consider next, how responses unfolded in that environment of real time shock and grief.

In the Sandy Hook community, there was an outpouring of love for each other. Neighbors looked out for neighbors, friends checked in on friends. Each taking turns being the giver and the receiver of comfort as shock turned to grief and other unfamiliar emotions. We saw beautiful

human care and support as parents and volunteers packed up and moved the entire school to a neighboring town's school that stood vacant, so that the students would not need to return to the place of the tragedy. "We are Sandy Hook. We Choose Love" was the motto quickly adopted by all who lived there.

Those living outside of the community also wanted to help. Seeing the images and hearing the stories on cable news and social media was more than many could bear. They couldn't sit idle and felt they needed to do something. Anything. This reaction drove hundreds of thousands of people to respond in a way that they *thought* would be helpful but was really *not* helpful. Those hundreds of thousands of people sent "things". In all, 65,000 stuffed animals were sent to a town of 27,000. There were nine tractor-trailers full of paper snowflakes, and half a million letters. That does not even count bikes, books and toys. It took years and thousands of volunteer hours to sort this out and find homes for all these "help" items.

Dr. Erika Doss, professor of American Studies at Notre Dame wrote a book on this emerging phenomenon entitled Memorial Mania. She talks about how we as a nation have become so attached to "things" that they provide meaning to us. Therefore, people send random "things" and expect them to be taken seriously.

I watched this phenomenon with awe and still grapple to come to terms with it. So

many people thinking they are helping are unknowingly adding to the burden of a community struggling to cope.

Random acts of kindness are a beautiful thing. Truly. But when you are in need of comfort, "random" is rarely helpful. A random "thing" sent to no one in particular can't take the place of an intentional one to one connection with someone who is caring just for you. Imagine if we could hit the rewind button and return those 65,000 stuffed animals and other random toys back to their senders and ask them to act intentionally and find someone in their own community to comfort in person. One to one. Face to face. Heart to heart. Hundreds of thousands of hurting people would feel seen, loved and comforted.

Comfort is a Long Term Undertaking

Long after the "helpful things" are cleaned up and the media trucks have moved on to the next tragedy, comfort and support are needed. It's when the chaos and busyness slows down that people really begin to face the pain.

A year after the tragedy as I was scrolling through my Facebook feed, I read this post from a friend in Sandy Hook. It sums up how many in this community were thinking:

"Good in a crisis? May be adrenaline, instinct. Good in the aftermath? Harder. Staying true to SHS but also yourself. Honoring in a way

When the chaos and busyness slows down– that's when people really begin to face the pain.

that is service, not self-serving....Knowing when to speak out, when to stay quiet. Our town is trying. I am trying."

There is no easy long term solution to a mass trauma. There is no playbook, there are no "one size fits all" guidelines. As of the writing of this book, it's almost 7 years after that tragic day and this same question is still being asked: "Now What?".

I knew in my heart the importance of being there long term because I too asked myself that same question every day: "Now what?" That's what drove me to show up week after week for 5 years. And it was the sum of responding to that question for those 5 years that really helped me to understand this elusive skill we call comforting.

In August of 2017 my husband took a new job and our family needed to relocate Virginia. It was not a move I was very excited about and so the roles of comforting were now reversed. I was the one that needed comfort and it was now that I would experience receiving comfort from those I had comforted for 5 years. Through all of the sad farewells, I realized something that I hadn't really paid much attention to before. Comforting is not about any one gesture at one time. Comfort is lots of little things that all add up. It's like filling up a jar with marbles - every marble added is cumulative to creating a full jar. Each time we connect with someone needing comfort, a marble is added to their jar. One connection = one marble. Little by little I had added countless marbles to many jars over those 5 years.

A beautiful journal was given to me at a farewell party with notes from the teachers and staff at SHS:

"Your smile was ever present at a time when we didn't have one. Greeting us with strong hugs every day, listening to us rage at the world, absorbing our anger and sadness."

"I truly hope that you know the impact that you had on my life and on the lives of my beloved SHS family. I can think of so many times when you could turn a moment around from deep sadness to a sense of peace. You taught me that sometimes just showing up is all that is needed to show someone that you care. That in the hardest of times I should hold on to what is good and that a simple hug can be the best medicine of all for a hurting heart,"

"You played a very big role in making school feel friendly and safe again and you became a dear dear friend".

There it was. The beautiful circle of comfort. The comforter becoming the comforted. The culmination of hundreds of little actions. Never one thing and at no one time. It was laying the foundation of trust and friendship, one connection of comfort at a time. And once that foundation is down, it is solid.

> Comforting is not about any one gesture at one time. Comfort is lots of little things that all add up.

What exactly did I do for those 5 years? Nothing you can't do yourself. It's simple and it doesn't even take your brain. It's all heart. I did this:

I raised my hand, I followed my heart and the voice that said "go".

I abandoned my desire to know exactly what happened

I took one step at a time each and every day.

Collected my things.

Got in the car.

Drove there.

Parked.

Prayed before I walked in.

I didn't let my uncertainty show.

Walked in with a smile.

Walked in with love.

Looked at everyone around me.

Made eye contact with everyone. The lunch ladies. The custodians. Everyone.

Asked them "how is today". And listened to their response. Just listened.

I offered no advice. Just listened and loved.

I hugged them. Always and often. Unless they didn't like hugs.

When I saw them again, asked them again: "how is today". And listened to their response. I didn't anticipate their response – every minute and day was different.

I was prepared for anything.

I helped with their daily tasks – great conversation happens over cleaning up a classroom.

I always tried to be warm, approachable and open with my body language.

I was confidential in all matters. I held their words as sacred and privileged.

Repeat. I kept coming back. Day after day. Week after week. I didn't disappear.

If I was invited to something, I went. You never know how important that invite is.

I was always available to them outside of the school day.

I introduced other people that came to help slowly.

I didn't leave them.

After some time, I was accepted as one of their privileged community. I didn't rush this, I didn't assume that would happen.

I'm still connected with them.

I celebrate with them their victories.

I cry when they cry.

I cherished the privilege of being there and with them. I always will.

In their shattered world, those hurting the most didn't need "stuff". They needed people to see them and to be there, and accept them for who they were. To acknowledge the difficulty that they were dealing with and give them the feeling of being understood. Day after day. Week after week. Month after month. Year after year. They needed love, acceptance, validation and understanding.

What they needed is what we all need and that is what you will learn in the rest of the book. Breaking through whatever is "your awkward" so that you can be the one that is there with friendship and understanding.

FEELING AWKWARD? YOU ARE NOT ALONE

I have long encouraged people to bring their whole selves to work but now my "whole self" was just so freaking sad. As hard as it was to bring up Dave with friends, it seemed even more inappropriate at work. So I did not. And they did not. Most of my interactions felt cold, distant, stilted. Walking around the Faceook campus, I started to feel like a ghost, somehow frightening and invisible at the same time.

SHERYL SANDBERG, OPTION B.

I still remember the very few teachers and other students who said "I'm sorry" after my older brother (a troubled student) was killed in a car accident 2 days before Christmas. But I also remember that almost no one said anything because the were uncomfortable or "didn't want to make me sad."

C. CARTER, **SOCIAL MEDIA POST**

I SEE PEOPLE AS THEY APPROACH ME, TRYING TO MAKE UP THEIR MINDS WHETHER THEY'LL "SAY SOMETHING" ABOUT IT OR NOT. I HATE IT IF THEY DO AND IF THEY DON'T.

–C.S. LEWIS

When my son was diagnosed with cancer many of my acquaintances would ask how he was doing. But my dearest friend avoided the topic entirely. One day while I was with her an acquaintance asked about him. I was trying to remain upbeat and began my story of how well he was doing when I noticed my friend turn away. At first I was angry until I saw her wipe tears from her eyes. I think she was in so much pain for me and my family and the young man she watched grow up, that she couldn't talk to me about it.

What I originally thought was not caring enough, turned out to be caring too much. I think sometimes we have to understand that those who love us are suffering also. This became even more obvious to me when I recently lost one of my dearest friends. Another friend who knew how close we had been embraced me and said how sorry she was for my loss. We usually reserve that sentiment for relatives. I think it's important to recognize that grieving isn't reserved just for the Immediate family.

ANONYMOUS

The Awkward Zone™ is the place where you want to help a person who is struggling, but don't know what to say or do.

WHAT IS THE
AWKWARD ZONE?

IDENTIFYING THE AWKWARD ZONE

The opportunity to enter the awkward zone begins the moment you learn of someone going through a hard time. At that moment you have a choice. You can avoid being awkward by taking the easier option of doing nothing or by carrying out a simple act of kindness. On the other hand, you can take the harder but more courageous choice. By embracing the awkward zone and pushing through your personal barriers, you can give meaningful comfort to someone one to one.

HOW DOES THIS PLAY OUT IN YOUR LIFE?

It's personally worth it to push through these challenges because when you do, you will make a real difference in someone's life which in turn will make a difference in your own. How this plays out in your life:

1. EVERYDAY LIFE

People's lives are moving at a noticeably faster pace. They can be complicated. Technology usage has a way of absorbing us into our own world and can distract us from people all around us who are struggling. It's a busy nonstop cycle that we get caught up in.

2. MISFORTUNES OCCUR

There is that moment when you hear of "what happened" or notice someone struggling. It happens anywhere and anytime on any given day. It's what you do next that matters.

3. YOU HAVE A CHOICE AS TO HOW YOU RESPOND:

DO NOTHING

Many fall into the "empathy/action gap". Wanting to do something but not taking action. This does nothing for those in pain and in reality only adds to their burden. Some are unaware and others simply don't care. Awkward is avoided here.

DO SIMPLE ACTS OF KINDNESS

When tragic news is still fresh we can feel the urgency to do something. Anything. Some options are a simple "click away" like giving money to a go fund me account. These actions allow the sender to feel better that they have helped. Some of these actions are good and some are needed. But if these acts are random and aren't followed up with checking in one to one, they are most often void of human connection and comfort. Awkward is avoided here.

FACE THE AWKWARD AND GIVE ONE TO ONE COMFORT

For most of us, connecting one to one with someone in pain is hard. That's why we call this the Awkward Zone. To reach those in pain, you must pause. Pause to remember them, to think about what they need and identify the barriers stopping you from reaching out. Pause to come up with strategies that work for you to intentionally connect one to one with that person so they know they are not alone. And then checking in - again and again and again. (More on these strategies in sections 3 & 4)

"Avoiding the Awkward Zone leads to missed opportunities to connect with those in need, and inadvertently makes the lonliness epidemic worse."

THREE IMPORTANT TAKEAWAYS FROM THE AWKWARD ZONE:

1. COMFORT IS INTENTIONAL

It's never random. When you feel impacted by a loss or tragedy - pause, review your choices of response and find the right person to intentionally reach out to, one to one.

2. IT'S NOT ABOUT YOU

Giving comfort means moving your focus to someone else. It may not always pay you back in the moment nor should it since that's not the point. Comfort is a long term undertaking that will eventually come back to you. You just don't know when. (see circle of comfort page 104)

3. ANYONE CAN DO THIS!

We all can break through the Awkward Zone - its about growing our awareness and then responding in many small ways. Giving lot's of marbles.

You are about to learn how to break it down, move beyond the Awkwardness and conquer this Awkward Zone!

20 AWKWARD BARRIERS TO COMFORT YOU CAN OVERCOME

There are real barriers to comfort. Recognizing these barriers and knowing you can break them down is key to comforting. In this section, we draw awareness to the barriers that stop so many of us from comforting others so that you can learn to work through them, change your behavior and move forward with giving comfort.

1. IT'S UNCOMFORTABLE

It does not come naturally to me. Most of us feel unable to comfort. But with practice, we can take the "un" out of uncomfortable

2. WAITING FOR THE PERFECT MOMENT

Putting it off because we are waiting for the perfect thing to do at the perfect time. "I'll wait to send or do the perfect thing when the time is right". Ultimately, nothing is ever done because we get busy and forget. Good intentions, but lack of follow through.

3. FEAR

The biggest barrier - fear of more pain or rejection. "I don't want to make it worse" "I'm afraid I'm not a good enough friend", "Maybe they don't want to hear from me", "I'm afraid to bring it up, it might ruin their day" "I think they just want to be with their close friends & Family."

4. IT TAKES EFFORT!

Of course we WANT to help, but actually taking the steps to *do* something feels like extra work in our already busy lives. It takes time and energy to comfort. So sometimes we just don't want to do it.

5. GROUP THINK

Being afraid to do something different from the rest of the crowd. "My friends don't think it's a good idea", "I don't want to do something that no one else is doing."

6. AVOIDANCE & APATHY

When we ignore the person struggling. We are all so busy and can fill our time so that we don't even have to give this person's pain a second thought. "I told them I would pray for them and then completely forgot.

7. SELF ABSORPTION

When we can't see past our own life to help others. We think that we will be fulfilled when we fill our lives with more things we want, when in fact it is the helping of others that we find the most fulfillment.

8. PASSIVITY

Assuming someone else can and will do it better - "I'm really not very good at this. There are others that are much better at knowing what to do. They have it covered."

9. GUILT

When you're not on good terms. "I had a fight with this person right before this happened, but in the scheme of things, it was petty."

10. REGRET

When you feel it's too late. It's been months and I haven't reached out. It's too late now. I'm embarrassed and I wish I would have done something sooner.

11. THEY ARE DIFFERENT FROM ME

When we dismiss reaching out to certain individuals because of their beliefs, lifestyle or social circle. If we neglect helping someone simply because of a group of people they mostly identify with.

12. LACK OF AWARENESS

Assuming people are ok and have moved on - "I think they are over it, they seem fine." "It's been over 6 months now, things should be getting back to normal." "They need to move on and get back to normal"

13. IT FEELS OVERWHELMING

When you don't feel that you can handle those extra emotions right now. "I'll get pulled down into the pit with them".

14. FEELING UNAPPRECIATED

When you feel your efforts go unnoticed. There is a saying out there "hurting people hurt people". Sometimes people who are hurting can vent to you and you feel that there is nothing you can do to help them. Additionally you feel that all of your efforts go unnoticed. Please don't fall into this trap. They need you. Fight through it. Your relationship will be stronger because of it.

15. DISPOSABLE FRIENDS & FAMILY

When you feel like it's more work than its worth. We are living in a fast paced disposable society and sometimes it seems that people treat their friends and family like they do their cars. If it's broken I'll just get another one. This doesn't work with comforting. It's in fighting through the hard times together that we find the most comfort of all.

16. NOT IN CONTROL OF TIMING

When you're not ready. "I saw my friend in the grocery story and I froze. I just didn't know what to say and was afraid I would say the wrong thing, so I avoided talking to her.

17. DESIRE TO FIX IT

Our desire to solve problems is a huge barrier in comforting and in listening. "If they would just listen to me" we think. When we move past this, comforting becomes so much easier.

18. YOU KNOW HIM BETTER

When asking friends how someone is doing fills your need to do anything. It's almost like checking in to see how a person is doing completes the comfort cycle for you. This does nothing for the one who is hurting.

19. LACK OF KNOWLEDGE

When you have no clue what to do. "I want to do something, but really just don't know what to do."

20. CAREGIVING FATIGUE

When you've reached the end of your helping rope. "I just don't know what to do anymore. It's been so long, and I've tried everything to help them. I'm exhausted and I just don't feel like helping anymore"

WHEN WE DON'T COMFORT: THE PRICE WE PAY IN THE WORKPLACE

"Our understanding of biology, psychology and the workplace calls for companies to make fostering social connections a strategic priority. A more connected workforce is more likely to enjoy greater fulfillment, and engagement while being more protected against illness, disability and burnout".

–Dr. Vivek Murthy Former Surgeon General

As Christa Carone and "Bananagate" demonstrated, and the trends in the last section have shown, the workplace is now one of our main centers of social connection. It's becoming the place where many people find their "tribe" so to speak. We used to think of work as just work. Go in do your job and go back to your life when you punch the clock on the way out the door. That's all changing. And as many of our daily connections have turned from face to face to screen, the workplace is still a place where face to face interactions are the norm, so thus the social hub.

Many of you reading this have a job or have had a job in the past. So you know how it feels when you get along with you co-workers or colleagues . You are happier, get more done and the team does higher quality work. There's less gossip and arguing, meaning less conflict and less turnover. We feel appreciated and cared for. When we're happy in the office, we're committed to our jobs and the company

we work for. Simple as that. We all know how important work relationships are.

But these relationships are also complicated.

Loneliness and isolation in the workplace is growing. The expanding use of social media for our friendships spills into the office and can result in a lack of workplace camaraderie. Office friendships are not as easy to form as people stay on their screens. Many employees will show up each day having been on their phones, computers and netflix with very little human interaction since they left the office the day before. Reduced face to face social engagement can lead to higher levels of competition, lack of transparency and reduced team cooperation. People that live lonely lives outside of work feel even more isolated in the office if they don't find friendships. Reduced connectedness is linked to low loyalty and low commitment to an organization. Lonely workers tend to view their co-workers as untrustworthy, this then hinders them from forming and maintaining important relationships as work, such as friendships or connections.

When employees feel alone and isolated in their pain, their productivity will suffer.

A LOOK BEHIND THE SCENES IN OUR WORKPLACES TODAY

Remember Keith from page 48? He's in a difficult situation, his colleagues are resentful for having to take on his work, no one has reached out to him to check in and he is pretty isolated from his team.

Keith, 32, Sales Manager

"I walked back into work and still hadn't told anyone that my Dad had committed suicide. Suicide! The word has such a sting to it and I still have not come to grips with why my Dad did it and my emotions are all over the place. I'm struggling.

I started noticing people looking at me differently, the sideways glances, no eye contact, nothing more than a quick "good morning", from anyone. I remember thinking they all know and they just want to know "what happened", what are the details. To me, all of that is just too painful. If they do say something to me, most people ask about my Mom. "How is she? It must be so hard for her", they say. They usually don't ask how I'm doing and so I go back to my office and try to make sense of the work on my desk. But I just can't.

I notice Sally in the accounting department has tears in her eyes most times I run into her. She always looks

> When employees feel alone and isolated in their pain, their productivity will suffer.

COMFORT IN THE WORKPLACE
EVERYONE IS IMPACTED BY MISFORTUNE.

Unfortunately, most people are unaware or just don't care

There is a large group of people who are so busy with their own lives that they pay no attention to those needing comfort. It would help them to be made aware of how to open their eyes to those struggling and learning simple ways to show that they care.

Then there are those who want to help but feel disconnected or don't know how

Often times when a life changing event happens to an employee there are many who want to help. They just don't know what to do. There is a real opportunity to facilitate caring connections in this group and allow them to do more than bring in things or money to help.

Close friends & colleagues can feel isolated

When a traumatic event happens to a close friend and colleague at work, they can feel ignored and isolated. As we see with Carol in the story on the next page, her motivation and desire to be at work decreases as she feels misunderstood and alone in her pain.

Unrecognized Sufferers may need support as a result of an additional trauma

There is a growing group of people in the workplace with unknown burdens and mental health issues. They come into work faking it every day. When these unrecognized sufferers are not attended to, they will eventually need much more support themselves.

Where most or all support is currently given

Closest friends & family

Employee Assistance Plan

Professional help

Outside Support

The Human Resource department has always been the epicenter of help for the employee going through a challenging time. This support many times also applies to the immediate family of the employee. Traditionally this is where the support stays.

like she wants to say something but never does. I have come to find out that her brother committed suicide a year ago. We haven't talked about it. It's awkward. "What will I say to her, what will she say to me?". So we both just put our heads down and get on with the day. Feeling more and more isolated and alone."

Keith's story is unfortunately more common than ever. He is talked about not directly to, there is a curiosity about "details" but not about his feelings. Even if someone musters the courage to say something to him, they ask about his Mom, not him. He can't focus on his work and knows he has to engage with the team again, but just doesn't know if he can do it. So he sits, letting another work day go by. Sally is an unrecognized sufferer in this scenario. Seeing Keith and knowing what has happened to his dad triggers her memories of her brothers suicide each and every time. Each alone in their grief.

Effect on his work:
Keith is isolating from his team and they are isolating from him. Without a cohesive team in place, most likely the entire team's work will suffer. Deadlines will be missed, mistakes will not be caught due to lack of communication and Keith's role of being the "sound board", will be vacant.

"I go back to my office and try to make sense of the work on my desk. But I just can't."

OTHER WORKPLACE SCENARIOS TO CONSIDER

Carol, 48, Office Manager

"Bob was my "work husband". Have you ever heard that term? It means that sometimes you meet someone at work, and you just connect. Not as a couple, but as a special friend and good trusted working partner. Everything worked better when Bob and I tackled a project together. We celebrated our successes and shared our frustrations at our failures. We were very close even though we didn't spend much time together outside of the office.

So when Bob died in the car accident that day, I was crushed. Not just sad, crushed. No more coffees in the break room, lunches comparing notes on our kids or our spouses. No more advice in getting through the office politics. And no more collaboration on the project that is due next week.

I think the entire office went to the funeral. When I saw Linda and the kids, I felt like I knew them all. When I went up to her, I wanted to hug her and tell her a million things, but all I could do was say "sorry for your loss". I was "just one of Bob's office people".

Back at the office, it seemed like everyone else moved on so quickly. We did a GoFundMe for Linda, we sent cards and dropped off food. But no one said anything to me. I missed him every day and I just felt a hole inside. I was super sad, but I didn't say anything to anyone and certainly no one said anything to me."

Carol is a "close friend and colleague" in the graph on page 89. All the support usually pours understandably to the closest family, but often there are others that are suffering too. Their grief is crippling, yet they have no one acknowledging their pain or feelings. They feel alone and misunderstood in their pain. Carol is also dealing with the sad truth that a large number in her workplace fall into the "unaware or just don't care". Their eyes are not open to others suffering as they are too busy dealing with their own life.

Effect on her work:
Carol is really struggling without her friend and confidant nearby. It can be assumed that Carol has a significant loss of focus as she grieves, and the group's needs might not be addressed with consequences in their productivity. She will most likely take more days off than normal as she processes feeling so alone in her grief.

Courtney, 26, Nurse Practitioner

"I'm just starting out in my career and I have worked very hard to finish school and start working. I love where I work, but I have just started so I feel all eyes are on me. To save money for my own place, I live with my parents because I can't afford my own rent yet.

When the house fire happened I was working and thankfully everyone got out safely. Even Boxer. My parents called and I rushed home, but by that time, we had lost everything. I had only the clothes on my back. A group of volunteers were at the scene and they set us up at a local hotel as we sat there lost and confused.

I somehow managed to get back to work and found that my co-workers had started a box of donations for my family. I thought that was so nice, but quickly realized that the box was filling up with things I didn't even feel like using. Old sheets and towels, used sweatshirts and dented cookie sheets. Everyone seems to want to help with their things instead of their hearts. Instead of asking how I am feeling through all of this, most will say things like "I'm so glad you're ok" and "Things can be replaced, thank God every one is ok and Boxer got out." But "we aren't o.k" I wanted to scream back - my life is upside down and inside out. But I don't because it truly seems like no one has the time or energy to take on my pain. So all I say is "Thank You"."

Courtney's situation is all too familiar. Even when a tragedy is visible like hers, the reaction is to set up a box for "things". Yes, she may need some things in this scenario, but what she really needed was someone to just be there with her in her confusion and despair. Yes, she was thankful everyone was o.k., but her current life situation was not. We often "judge" someone's situation to see how "bad" it is, and we donate our old items. But in doing so, we discount how people are reacting to what has happened to them, and what they truly need.

Effect on her work:
Without someone connecting with her and acknowledging that her loss was personal and that their donations of sheets were

not what she really needed, Courtney's productivity may suffer, causing serious ill effects.

Debbie, 35, Director of Sales, Fortune 50 company

"I am a mid level executive at a fortune 50 company. My performance is excellent and I'm due for a promotion. In fact, my performance is so good that I routinely win a spot on the coveted incentive trip each year awarded only to the very best performers in the company.

But this year, as the incentive trip nears, I wish I didn't have to go. In reality, I would prefer to take some extended time off work. You see, my marriage is crumbling and my kids and I have moved out of our family home and are living with my mom. I have a restraining order against my husband and fear for my kids and my own safety. Now more than ever, I need my job and so I don't want work to know what's going on. I'm afraid that if people knew what was going on in my life, they would question my character and think it was my fault I was in this situation. Or they might be concerned that I will be distracted from getting my work done. Both of these could impact my potential promotion. So I stay silent.

When the incentive trip rolls around, I know I need to go. After all, the pressure is now on me to support my kids so I must do everything I can to keep my career on track. Flying to a tropical island is torture. Each moment away from my kids brings me anxiety and fear. As I watch the rest of the attendees soak up the sun and relish each new adventure and party, every time I turn down a drink at the pool and stay away from the bars, I feel the eyes of the team on me. There is pressure to be a team player and participate. I really have no one to talk to and have never felt more alone."

This is the thing with this situation. There is zero chance that Debbie would ever default on her job responsibilities. She needs the job and she wants the job. It's her security and it's her sanity right now. She only needs understanding without judgement. It's really not too much to ask. But by not being able to be her genuine self with support and care from those around her, her internal conflict and anxieties soar. She is now a single mom without a home, her dream of a perfect marriage is shattered and she has lost her social structure. Her work is where she is spending the majority of her hours and feeling isolated in her own bubble of crisis.

Effect on her work:
Debbie is headed for burnout which is a serious and debilitating situation. The negative effects of hopelessness spill into every part of life - work, home, and relationships. Without her ability to be open and honest at her workplace and without her employer's support, Debbie may be in danger of losing her job and livelihood as well as her emotional stability.

Robert, 28, Guidance Counselor at private high school

"I have been "uneasy" all my life. I try to act casual and worry free, but I struggle from crippling anxieties. I have tried to be very honest and up front about it at the school

WHEN EMPLOYEES NEED COMFORT

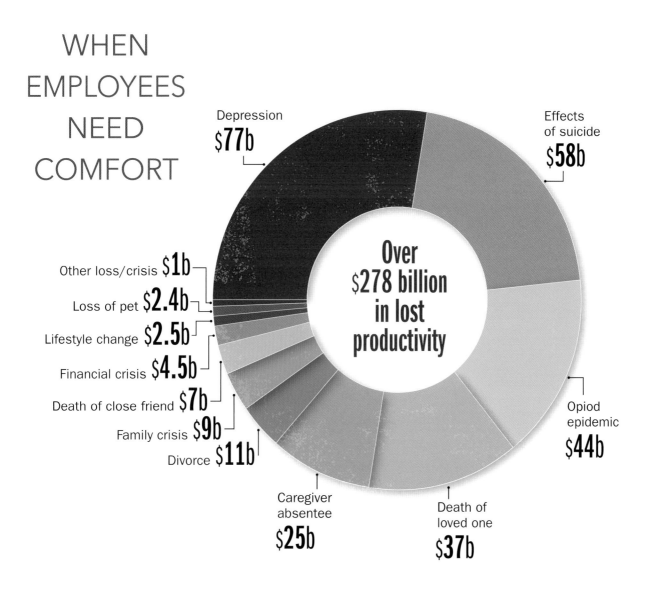

Depression
$77b

Effects of suicide
$58b

Other loss/crisis $1b

Loss of pet $2.4b

Lifestyle change $2.5b

Financial crisis $4.5b

Death of close friend $7b

Family crisis $9b

Divorce $11b

Over $278 billion in lost productivity

Opiod epidemic
$44b

Caregiver absentee
$25b

Death of loved one
$37b

Every single employee is someone's son or someone's daughter. Like a parent, a leader of a company is responsible for their precious lives.

~ SIMON SINEK

I work at and they tell me they understand but I don't think they do. I have to take sick days here and there but I can't help it. There are days I am frozen with fear and panic.

I get the feeling that my colleagues don't understand. They come in and try to "cheer me up" and tell me just to "pull up my boot straps" and get going. I feel guilty that they have to take on some of my case load when I'm out and that makes things even worse for me. They like to maintain a "happy" work environment for the students, but sometimes, I just can't. Some have even questioned whether or not I exaggerate how I feel. They have no idea what it's like to live with anxiety nor do they want to know what it's like and how they can help me. They are more comfortable talking about me than to me."

In Robert's case, his colleagues don't know what to say to him and may feel resentful to have to take over his work. They are the ones in the graph on page 89 that are "unaware or just don't care". They think whatever he has is overblown and he should just move past his feelings and get going. After all–they are all tired and overworked too.

Effect on his work:
Without an honest assessment of Robert's mental health, his colleagues are most likely complaining of their increased work load and will minimize his true situation. They are either unaware or just don't care what causes him to miss work, but they know it affects them and they make that known to their leaders.

Those who say they have no real friends at work have only a one in 12 chance of feeling engaged in their job.

Conversely, if you have a "best friend at work", you are seven times more likely to feel engaged in your job, according to Tom Rath, author of *Vital Friends: The People You Can't Afford to Live Without.*

As we saw in the earlier stories, people need meaningful connections from co-workers and staff just as they would from other close friends and family. When these needs aren't met, there are both quantifiable and qualifiable damages that can occur.

Lindsey Knerl, in her recent article, "Here's why mental health at work is everyone's business" says this, "..its important to create a work environment where people can offer each other support, and that can get difficult if they aren't aware of the issues their coworkers are facing. The best policy, in my opinion, is to foster a stigma-free environment that encourages staff to reach out for help, whether that be to HR, their manager, or a friendly coworker. Managers or HR should step in and offer help when they observe a team member who is engaging in dangerous behavior on the job or is emotionally impaired in a way that impacts their work."

The responsibility for creating positive workplace connections and relationships is not solely the responsibility of the HR department, a committee or a department head. It is up to each one of us in the workforce. Every single employee from the president down to a summer intern is capable of engaging with someone struggling. Whether in an elevator, in the lunchroom, over a text or right at their desk.

Not sure where to start? No worries, that is coming up next!

THE COST OF NOT CARING FOR THOSE NEEDING COMFORT IN OUR WORKPLACES & COMMUNITIES

The Founders of Inspiring Comfort, based on decades of experience as executives and then comforters, have found the following to be true: An employee who feels unsupported, misunderstood and/ or afraid to share key life events:

1. Is not as dedicated to his colleagues and manager

2. Is not as loyal to the organization

3. Is more likely to call in sick and take days off

4. Will not exceed expectations, has difficulty meeting expectations

and will most likely operate in a below expectations mode due to lack of concentration and impaired decision making.

5. May cause conflict and divisiveness because at the core of it all is the simple fact that hurting people, hurt people.

6. Gossip happens, rumors start and discorse reigns supreme.

7. Mangers will spend their time taking care of symptoms but not the root of the problem. Not able to offer solutions, only putting out fires.

It doesn't take the HR department to fix this. It's human interaction and caring and concern that is needed. And every one of us can learn how to do that better.

As we saw in our earlier stories, people need meaningful connections from co-workers and staff just as they would from other close friends and family. When these needs aren't met, there are both quantifiable and qualifiable results.

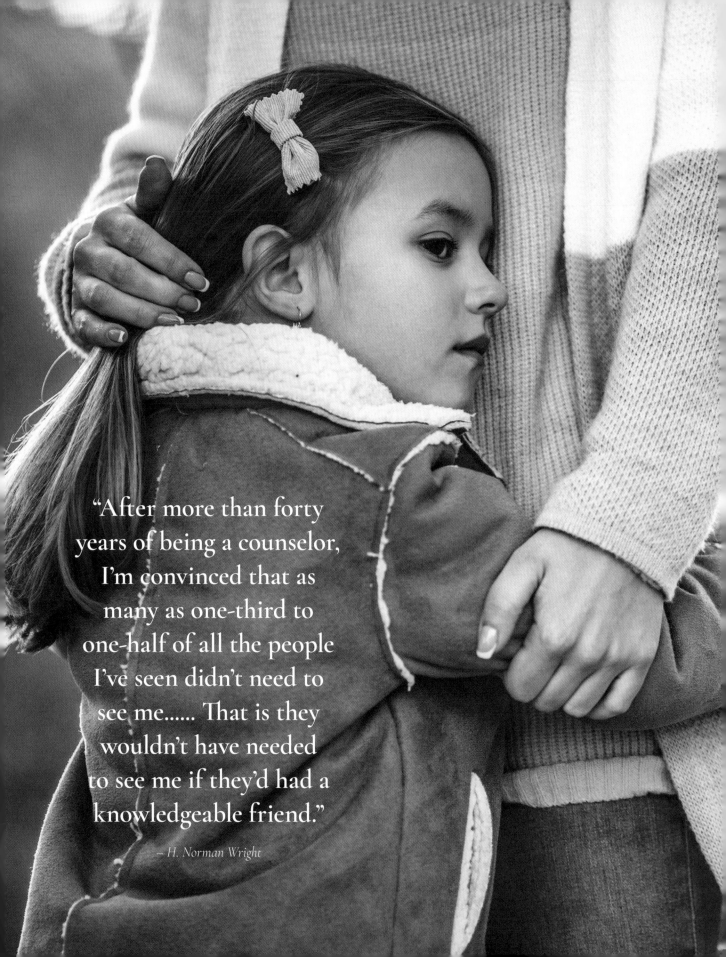

"After more than forty years of being a counselor, I'm convinced that as many as one-third to one-half of all the people I've seen didn't need to see me...... That is they wouldn't have needed to see me if they'd had a knowledgeable friend."

— *H. Norman Wright*

PART THREE

Learning
The Skill of
Comfort

Comfort: Why its more than just a word

The Circle of Comfort and the science behind it

Why do we give comfort: What's really going on

Who needs comfort? We all do!

Thinking differently: The need for comfort never ends

The powerful full body experience of giving comfort

Heart, ears, eyes, hands, feet & soul comfort

COMFORT [kuhm-fert]: WHY IT'S MORE THAN JUST A WORD

"People might forget what you said but they will never forget how you made them feel."

Comfort is one of those words with multiple meanings. Search "comfort" in a web browser and you will find comfort food, airline seats with more legroom, air conditioning units, fabric softener, shoes and mattresses among other things that make our lives more "comfortable". However, few of these "comforts of life" deal with the comfort we most crave.

Emotional comfort. Being comforted when we're hurt, suffering, broken, frustrated, grieving, anxious, depressed, stressed, fearful, lonely or isolated.

According to the dictionary comfort is "the easing or alleviation of a person's feelings of grief or distress". This is a very sterile and brainy description of an action that is not at all sterile or brainy. Comfort is all heart. It includes your time and your compassion. It's intentional and purposeful. It can't be bought.

Our world is now "connected" 24/7. But connecting with a screen is not connecting with a heart. Comfort is a perfect antidote to this "connected disconnection". It is an action, therefore it's a skill that can be learned. And it demonstrates genuine caring and connection where it counts the most: Face to face and heart to heart.

Comforting awakens our natural empathic response which the frantic, disconnected pace of life often buries. You slow down when you comfort someone, and you listen better. Relationships will deepen and your view of others will improve when you comfort them. Comfort includes kindness but goes much deeper than a random act. And a critical benefit of comforting is this: Your own heart will feel love and comfort when you comfort others.

The physical, emotional and social benefits of comfort are endless.

Comfort is an intentional action that comes from the heart. It carries with it many beautiful human qualities including empathy and compassion to form caring one to one connections.

THE CIRCLE OF COMFORT & THE SCIENCE BEHIND IT.

How does one actually relearn the skill of comfort? You learn by practicing.

Let's take a look at the process we developed at Inspiring Comfort for learning this critical skill through Sam's story.

Sam was a 6th grader who didn't much like being at school. He didn't have friends in his class and spent most of his time with his aide. After school, he preferred to go straight home and play video games. He definitely had no interest in joining an after-school club. However, his grandmother, whom he lived with, had other ideas. She signed Sam up to attend an Inspiring Comfort 8-week after-school program, Club Comfort.

You can imagine how excited Sam was to be there on the first session of the club. He was not only extremely uninterested in the club, he was downright rebellious and combative. He disrupted the first session shout-ing out things like "This is stupid" "I don't even want to be here". His aide, a wonderful woman who went to each class with him every day, came to his side and tried to encourage him to stay, but he was getting more and more agitated and both he and the other students were becoming uncomfortable. She whispered they would be leaving early, but would be back for the next session.

During the second session he sat outside of the circle of the other club participants with his aide. His arms crossed in defiance. He had a few outbursts but was not as disruptive as the first session and he was able to stay for the whole session. He did not pay much attention to the lesson nor did he participate in discussions. But he did stay and watch (with his arms crossed) and he did participate in the activity. Together

with his aide he identified someone who was in need of comfort, thought of a personal message and made a beautiful comfort plaque to be hand delivered.

By the fourth session - Sam sat with the group in the circle. Not participating in the discussions but his arms were no longer crossed and even more important, Sam - who did not like anything to do with school –had followed through on his in-club and take-home tasks since the second session.

By the Fifth Session – Sam walked into the classroom and asked if it was Club Comfort day. When he was told yes, he said "good".

By the Seventh Session - When the following question was posed to the group during that day's lesson: "how would you feel if you didn't get to see your family for a long time", Sam raised his hand and answered: "sad, disappointed, discouraged".

By the Eighth Session – Sam arrived early in the room and helped sort out the activity supplies. That was a wow. The group discussion that day focused on "Appreciative Comfort"–when those who help you don't feel appreciated, they can feel lonely and sad. The kids were prompted to think of people who help them but may not get much appreciation. Several kids answered with the names of family members, but that's not who we were looking for so we kept probing. And then it happened again. Sam's hand popped up and he offered up "The Janitor". The perfect answer. And that's who he chose to comfort that day.

Witnessing Sam move from combative to attentive to participating to initiating was one of the most amazing progressions I have ever witnessed in a withdrawn and isolated child. All in 8 short weeks.

How could that happen?

THE COMFORT PLAQUES

Our signature Inspiring Comfort plaque is a one to one connection of comfort created specifically by someone for someone. It carries a heartfelt message and creates a lasting keepsake of personalized encouragement

THE CIRCLE OF COMFORT

After working with thousands of kids like Sam, we began to document the process of what exactly was being done when you give comfort to someone. There are specific steps that if practiced and learned, bring about comfort. The more we work with this process, the more that the beauty and the magic of it are revealed. This process breaks us through the awkward zone. It works with any personality type and in any and all situations where people are needing care and support.

KIM AND ELLIE'S STORY

COMFORT COMING FULL CIRCLE

KIM

It was just over 6.5 years ago when my two youngest children were exposed to one of the worst acts of violence this country has ever seen, the Sandy Hook Elementary School tragedy. 12.14.12. Aidan was in 4th grade and Ellie was in 1st grade. While both of them were diagnosed with PTSD, Ellie's symptoms, especially in the early days were more "extreme" than Aidan's. Returning to school that following January was very challenging, especially for Ellie. She did not want to go to school at all and would beg to stay home. I knew there were Comfort Dogs waiting at the school, so would say each day, "Let's just go see the dogs and then we will take it from there." Receiving comfort got her back to school.

Little by little the initial support structures in our school were taken away. As counselors left and security was reduced we felt an overwhelming pressure in our school and community to move on. There was a common message we kept hearing that we weren't just going to be "survivors" we were going to be "thrivers". But what did that look like? How could we "thrive" when we were just trying to get through every day without a panic attack or break down of some sorts?

Giving comfort to others filled that void for Ellie and I. We learned this when we joined a Club Comfort that formed in our town. It gave us something positive to do and a community of like-minded girls and moms to gather with every month. Over soup and art, we catch up with each other is a safe environment where everyone belongs, and we intentionally focus on someone else's need for comfort. It was our turn to be able to comfort others after all of those months of being on the receiving end of comfort!

Club Comfort has become something that especially Ellie can't go without attending. If there is a scheduling conflict, she insists on prioritizing it over other activities. I can honestly say it is THE single most important activity that she has participated in and I believe there are a few reasons for this.

First, when you are spending time giving to others, you don't have time to focus on your own pain which lightens your burden. Additionally, incredible relationships have been born out of the Club. These relationships are more than just friendships because they have been bonded in something so truly meaningful. The love and support and friendships created continue to help Ellie and I throughout many areas of our lives.

In yet another layer of comfort, Ellie and I have started a Club Comfort at our church.

We want others to learn how incredible it feels to provide comfort to someone in need. And to round out our journey of comfort, Ellie will be receiving a service dog to assist her with her PTSD symptoms and anxiety.

Comfort will continue to pave our path forward each day.

ELLIE

I have always been a dog person. Mostly because of how they always know the right way to comfort me when I'm having a hard time. Even though they are dogs, just knowing that they care makes me happy. It is almost like a cycle. My dog comforts me and when a smile appears on my face, a smile appears on theirs. That is exactly what comfort is. A cycle.

I had a friend who I wasn't very close with but I heard that she was sick and in the hospital. I wanted to let her know that I was thinking about her and she was in my prayers. So, I thought I would make her a plaque. When I sent her the plaque I received letter back from her that said "thank you, that meant a lot to me". By making my friend a plaque, not only did it comfort my friend, but it also comforted me. Club Comfort is so important to me because it is a cycle of comfort. By comforting others I am comforted.

THE CIRCLE OF COMFORT

I reflect back on how helping this person helped me too

Participant

5. I REFLECT BACK

On myself - By helping someone else feel better, it can make you feel better. The action of doing something for someone lifts our mood and lets us forget our own hurts. Feel good chemicals are released in our brain.

On The Person I Comforted - What did we observe? What more do they need? We reflect on how this was one step, but an accumulation of many little things will bring this person even greater lasting comfort.

Connection/Observation

When we connect, I focus on them not me

Skill-based Learning

4. I CONNECT WITH THIS PERSON

We choose to focus on them, not ourselves. We offer our hearts, ears, love and time. We observe their reaction. There can be tears of thankfulness or other times hugs. The person comforted feels encouraged someone "saw" them. They feel special and loved.

Person Needing Comfort

Required Action

Participant

Self Identification

I take time to think of others

Situational Analysis

I choose to help someone hurting and find the right message

Overcoming Barriers

I intentionally reach out even if it's awkward

1. I TAKE THE TIME TO THINK OF OTHERS

The first step takes the focus off you. Put down your phone, step away from social media and think of all the people you know who are struggling.

2. I CHOOSE TO HELP SOMEONE

The intentional action is a commitment to help someone specific. Efforts aren't random. We connect with a specific person. Those who hurt can feel isolated and need one-to-one connection. Once a person is identified, we find the right message for them. Searching our hearts, remembering what they like and making them aware that you are there for them. Reaching them with specific messages of care and comfort so they don't feel alone.

3. I INTENTIONALLY REACH OUT

even if it's awkward – The intentional action is key to comfort. Often we fall into the "empathy action gap" - wanting to do something but failing to follow through. No one can feel your thoughts, but they can feel your actions. Kind thoughts are meaningless if they are not acted upon. In this step we break thru the Awkward Zone™.

TAKEAWAY

When we are hurting - when we have hard stuff in our life - giving comfort by reaching out to connect with someone else going through a hard time is the perfect medicine for giving ourselves hope. It's counterintuitive, as sometimes we view this as extra "work" we don't have time for. But by helping others, we will help ourselves. Every time.

That is a circle of comfort: you to someone, someone back to you. Comforting others doesn't take away your problems, but it does take the focus off your problems. By helping someone else through their struggles it brings the two of you closer together and your own problems begin to seem smaller.

THE SCIENCE BEHIND THE SKILL FIVE QUESTIONS WITH DR. DAVID DESTENO

A sit-down with Dr. David Desteno, professor of psychology at Northeastern University, and a fellow at the American Psychological Association.

How is Comfort an evidence based skill?

Most of us think we're compassionate. We think we'd step up to help someone in need when the time came. But what scientific research shows time and again is that people's beliefs about how they'll treat others doesn't often match their actions. When it comes to offering comfort, evidence matters. Questionnaires about what people intend to do don't mean much. What's convincing is seeing behaviors actually change -- seeing people take the initiative to reach out to help others in ways that can be dif-

ficult at times. Ways that are personal, that have connection, not just spending a few dollars and moving on. What impresses me about the work of Inspiring Comfort is the changes those who have gone through it report. They're spending time to connect with others, to have difficult conversations, to "be there" in ways that aren't always easy to do.

How is it that in helping others, we ourselves are helped?

For scientists, this has long been a question: Why should we help other people if it is difficult or costs us time, money, or other

other resources? The problem with that view is it betrays ignorance of the fact that humans are a social species. Over time, we gain from helping each other. Yes, it can be costly to go help someone in the short-term. Even giving them a shoulder to cry on can be difficult to handle emotionally. But time and again, what research shows is that those small costs tend to be repaid in greater amounts over time. When adversity strikes (and adversity always does), those who have extended compassion to others have a community ready and willing to support them in their own time of need. Building these social networks is so important to our wellbeing that our brains actually value giving help to others. When we do it, the brain's reward centers activate. Why? Because enhancing others' wellbeing is a down payment on enhancing our own.

Can you learn comfort even if you don't feel empathy or compassion in your heart?

Yes! And this is an extremely important fact to understand, empathy and compassion are skills. They're usually not innate, In fact, there's great research by a psychologist named Jamil Zaki at Stanford that shows simply getting people to believe that they can improve their empathy immediately makes them more

willing to comfort others. What I value so much about this approach to teaching comfort as a skill is its step-by-step focus on teaching skills to enhance empathy and removing barriers that inhibit it, all in a science backed way. One of the biggest reasons people don't engage in the sometimes difficult work of comforting others is that they feel ill-equippped. By teaching them how to deal with potentially awkward situations, how to reach out to others, how to step up and simply be there when needed, can help them to feel efficacious. And what decades of research shows is that feelings of efficaciousness are one of the biggest predictors for whether someone will engage in an activity. To try and do something challenging, we have to feel we have the tools. And the programs and workshops Inspiring Comfort is building, including this book Paws to Comfort, are built around exactly that: giving people the tools they need to comfort others.

Why is it important to focus on a specific person to help while learning comfort instead of sending something randomly?

For most of our evolutionary history, humans interacted face-to-face. There was no internet; there was no Amazon. We couldn't simply hit a button to send some

"Enhancing others' wellbeing is a down payment on enhancing our own."

money or a teddy bear to children in need. So now, when we attempt to comfort others in this way, there's a big miscalibration and motivation problem. Without truly coming to know the person we're trying to comfort, it's difficult to know what they truly need. Backing up the point, there's a good deal of research to show that the help and gifts people most appreciate aren't a function of cost, but rather a function of thought. Did someone spend the time to figure out what I need? If so, it is very affirming and comforting. If not, it's a throw-a-way. But an even bigger problem than miscalibration is motivation. When we send $20 or a stuffed animal by clicking a button, we lose that personal interaction. When I mentioned above that our brains' reward circuits are attuned to giving to others, that means giving in a way where this a social interaction - a way where we can see the joy and comfort those sacrifices bring to the people we're trying to help. If we don't get that feedback, it can become difficult to keep on comforting. It's for these reasons that I would urge people, at least at the start, to focus on helping individuals with whom they can interact. That's the way to train your brain, so to speak, to learn the value that is intrinsic to comforting others.

Is it good for us to focus on helping someone else through their struggles even when we have our own?

Yes, but with a caveat. This is one of the questions that my research group has been investigating for awhile. In work led by my colleague Daniel Lim, what we find is that those who have suffered their own adversities in life and successfully come through them are more ready to offer comfort to others. In fact, one primary reason why they do so is that they feel they know how to help. Having lived through adversity themselves, they realize how important receiving comfort from others was to them and how even seemingly small acts can make an important difference. What this work suggests is that focusing on teaching comforting skills is essential. For those who have been fortunate enough not to have faced significant adversity in their lives, learning the comforting skills that others have developed via more trying experiences, can be a major step in enabling their ability to empathize. But now for the caveat: it can be difficult to comfort others when you're in the throes of distress yourself. When you're suffering, let others comfort you. It's important to remember that when it comes to the circle of comfort, being willing to accept is as important as being willing to give. Along the road of life, there will be times when people need to do one or the other. The trick to living a good life is to be able to do both.

Dr. David DeSteno is a professor of psychology at Northeastern University and the author of "Emotional Success: The Power of Gratitude, Compassion, and Pride."

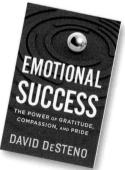

The Scientific Benefits Of Comfort

FIVE KEY TAKEAWAYS
FROM DR. DAVID DESTENO

Mutual Benefits

Enhancing others' well being is a down payment on enhancing our own.

Learning Empathy

Comfort can be learned even in those who lack empathy.

Thoughtful Gifts

Research indicates that the help and gifts people most appreciate aren't a function of cost, but rather a function of thought.

Personal Interaction

DeSteno urges people to focus on helping individuals with whom they can interact. People can train their brain to learn the intrinsic value of comforting others.

Recieving Comfort

Being willing to accept comfort is as important as being willing to give it. Along the road of life, there will be times when people need to do one or the other. The trick to living a good life is to be able to do both.

WHY DO WE COMFORT: WHAT'S REALLY GOING ON

You meet thousands of people and none of them really touch you. And then you meet one person and your life is changed forever. - Unknown.

When we think back to the the story of Sam in the last section, there is another back story that needs to be told.

Sam came in to that group beaten down and hurting. Turns out Sam no longer lives with his Mom who has a history of mental illness and a sister who is also often hospitalized with addiction struggles. Because of this instability, Sam lives full time with his Grandma who is doing the very best she can. He has difficulty regulating his emotions and filtering his thoughts and words. He goes through his school day with an assigned aide in an attempt to help him get through the day and stay in class. Having difficulty with emotions and prone to verbal outbursts, he is left without a friend group - isolated,

sad, frustrated and angry. You can imagine the gremlins he faces in his head each and every minute of each and every day. In an attempt to help, his Grandma signed him up for this after school group - he had no choice, he had to attend.

Like so many in our world today who feel like they have no place where they really "belong" or are lacking purpose, Sam also needed to feel like he belonged as a first step. In order for him to progress from combative to attentive to participating to initiating, he needed to feel that he could trust his setting and those around him. He needed a place where people wouldn't laugh at him or bully him. And he needed to know that his help and insight would be valued by everyone present.

CORE HUMAN TRUTHS

According to Leadership guru John Maxwell, there are core human truths and basic needs that are the foundation of every relationship and every interaction we have with each other. Every single person we interact with, on every level of our lives wants to be:

* Safe

* Seen

* Have a sense of trust

* Valued

* Known

* Heard

* Touched

* Assured of hope

They:

* Are insecure

* Are hurting

* Want to be understood

* Lack direction

* Are needy

* Need encouragement

* Want to feel that you see them as someone unique & special

* Desire relationships & community

Sam		The Janitor
GIVER OF COMFORT		**RECEIVER OF COMFORT**

EMPATHIC RESPONSE		CORE HUMAN VALUE TOUCHED
I've noticed that the janitor seems very forgotten. He helps us every day but no one ever says hi to him and appreciates what he does.	**Paws to Look See Remember**	I'm alone in my pain. No one sees me. I don't feel like I belong anywhere.
I wonder what would make the janitor feel like people like him. He always wears a Packer hat and likes to whistle. He must love football.	**Paws for Thought**	I'll bet no one even cares how I feel. I don't like living alone and then coming here and feeling alone. The only thing that keeps me sane is watching football but then I argue with other fans online.
I'm going to create something to give to him. I'm going to thank him for making my school clean and for always smiling and cheering me up.	**Paws to Create**	I wish I had more to look forward to each day.
I know he is always in the cafeteria at lunch time. I'm going to bring my gift of comfort to him then. I'm nervous but I think it will make him happy.	**Paws to Give / Connect**	Wow. I had the best day today. One of the students made me the kindest gift. Just for me. It was this little wooden plaque. It was yellow and he made a packer logo and put a football on it with the words "Never give up". On the back he wrote a note to me how he appreciated me keeping the school clean and how he liked my whistling. I can't believe it. Someone took the time to see me and care. I haven't felt this good in a long time. What a special kid.
Wow. He loved my plaque! When I told him why I made this for him I saw that he had tears in his eyes. He told me that he will put the plaque on his dresser so that he always remembers how kind the world can be. Next time I see him I want to ask him if he's ever actually gone to Lambeau field for a Packer game. He was so nice.	**Paws to Reflect**	Coming to work today was easier. I felt seen and appreciated. I felt like I made a difference in someone's life and that was great. I want to make sure to thank Sam again. I'll look for him at lunch and share with him once again how much his plaque meant to me.

THE SIX BASIC COMFORT PROGRAM RULES

While we were developing our Inspiring Comfort programs, it was important for us to set up programming that creates an environment where everyone can thrive, especially people like Sam. So we created our basic comfort program rules to allow each participant to "give permission" to themselves and to others. To be open to learn and open to comfort. After all the most effective learning happens in an environment that is grounded in our human values. An atmosphere of trust, security and belonging. For every session we teach and every program we run, we emphasize these points. Every single time. For most students we even ask them to sign a document to show that they understand and agree to these rules when they participate.

1. EVERYONE BELONGS
No one is unworthy. No one is different in what we are trying to accomplish. We all belong here.

2. WE HAVE ALL MADE MISTAKES
We've all messed up. No one is perfect. We've done things we regret. Start fresh. Forget the past and instead look ahead to all of the good you can do.

> "To add value to others one must first value others."
>
> *–JOHN MAXWELL*

3. WE ASSUME THE BEST IN EACH OTHER
Every day with every person we interact with, we have a choice. We can assume the best in that person, or we can assume the worst. It's not ok to assume the worst in someone, so here we will always assume the best.

4. WE SUPPORT AND CARE FOR EACH OTHER
When we assume the best in each other, the next natural step is to support and care for each other. When we work together, we will help and support each other when we are having a hard time.

5. WE WILL CHOOSE TO MAKE A DIFFERENCE IN THE LIVES OF OTHERS
Here we have another choice. We can spend our lives focused on ourselves and our needs, or we can choose to help others. The truth is, when we help others, we help ourselves. So that's what we do.

6. WE WILL TAKE OWNERSHIP AND BE PROUD OF WHAT WE ARE DOING
If others try to make fun of what we are doing or ridicule us, we will not agree, and we will not engage. Instead we will stand up for what is right.

When Sam signed these program rules on day one and re-read them at the start of each session, his walls gradually broke down.

WHAT GOES ON WHEN WE COMFORT

When we want to comfort someone, we start here. We focus on them and not us. And at some point the Receiver of Comfort will become a Giver of Comfort and a new circle of comfort begins.

THE GIVER OF COMFORT

1. Is intentional in looking to see the basic human needs of a person

2. Is focused on the needs of the other

3. Is concentrating on saying or doing something that will bring this person comfort

4. Is aware in seeing what more this person might need

5. Is feeling comforted by comforting someone as their empathic system engages.

6. Is reflecting more and more that life is not about ME.

7. Is realizing that a friendship is beginning or is deepening.

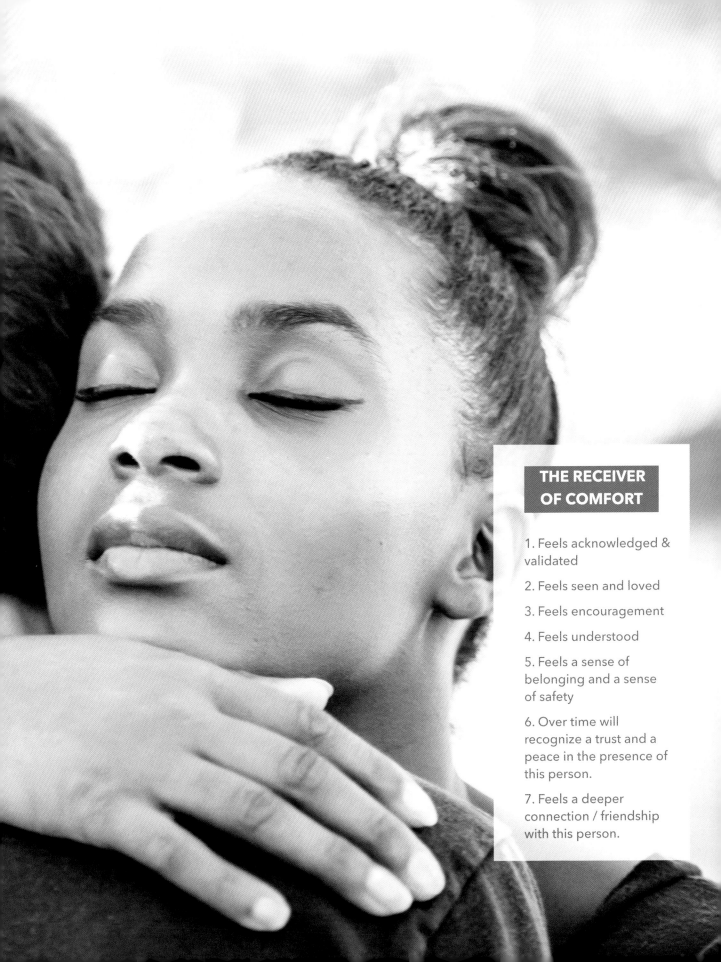

THE RECEIVER OF COMFORT

1. Feels acknowledged & validated

2. Feels seen and loved

3. Feels encouragement

4. Feels understood

5. Feels a sense of belonging and a sense of safety

6. Over time will recognize a trust and a peace in the presence of this person.

7. Feels a deeper connection / friendship with this person.

WHO NEEDS COMFORT? WE *ALL* DO.

Everyone you know has a problem you may or may not know about. Macro and micro stressors add to all of our daily burdens.

I was facilitating the first session of one of Inspiring Comfort's after school clubs with a group of middle schoolers when I saw two very shy kids paired up for an activity. It was a simple "get to know you" session and I was worried that they wouldn't be able to initiate conversation as they both looked very uncomfortable. So I asked if they wanted help and they said yes. I started by asking Shannon, "Is there any reason you would like to be cheered up today?" And with that one simple question, she burst into tears. It was unexpected to say the least but she answered, "My step sister just moved away and I have no idea if and when I'll ever see her again." At this point, Colin, the shy boy, immediately started asking her questions like "Where did she move to? How old is she?" Shannon answered them which surprised me. Colin then asked her "What makes you happy?"

and she answered "rainbows, panda bears and the color purple". Shannon then asked Colin if he needed to be cheered up and he replied "I get picked on because I'm not athletic". He liked pokemon.

They went on to make each other incredibly caring comfort plaques. She made him a Pokemon plaque that said "Be Brave & Be Strong". He made her a purple rainbow plaque that said "Hang in there" and drew a panda on the back. They each wrote the other a beautiful message of encouragement on the back. By the end of the session they were happy and talking to each other.

Two students, who most likely never would have even talked to each other, were paired up in a trusting environment and given confidence that it was safe to share. Someone saw their pain and was simply there to listen. In the end they felt understood and a sense of belonging. This is the process of human connection which changes lives. This is comfort.

So many people today have a hurt so deep and so close to the surface that even the simplest of caring questions will open up a floodgate of emotions. So our journey of comfort needs to start in building awareness. Opening our eyes to those around us who are hurting and may not even show it. We need to "Paws" and look, seeing those in pain and remembering those who we know are struggling.

GROWING OUR AWARENESS

There is a saying out there, "If you care, you'll be aware". And that's really it in a nutshell. We have a choice every day with every single action we take to see life not through our own eyes, but through the lens of the person we are interacting with. That cashier at the gas station that is short with you? She has some medical tests this afternoon that she is anxious about. Your coworker who has been late to work every day this week? She's caring for her aging mother with Alzheimers and is facing life with a mother who no longer recognizes her.

When you realize that every person you interact with is dealing with something, you begin to look at people and life differently. We start to realize that life is really about doing it together and not alone. When we help others through their struggles, they will help us through our own.

We're in this thing called life together and it's way better when we comfort each other through it.

THOUGHTS ON COMFORT

I never got the question in my first five years at USC that I now get almost daily from students: "How do I make friends?" Students may have thousands of friends online, but few in real life; they may be experts at talking with their thumbs, but not so much with their tongues. As a result, many feel as though they don't have a tribe or a sense of belonging. They feel disconnected from what it means to be human.

–VARUN SONI,
Dean of religious life, USC

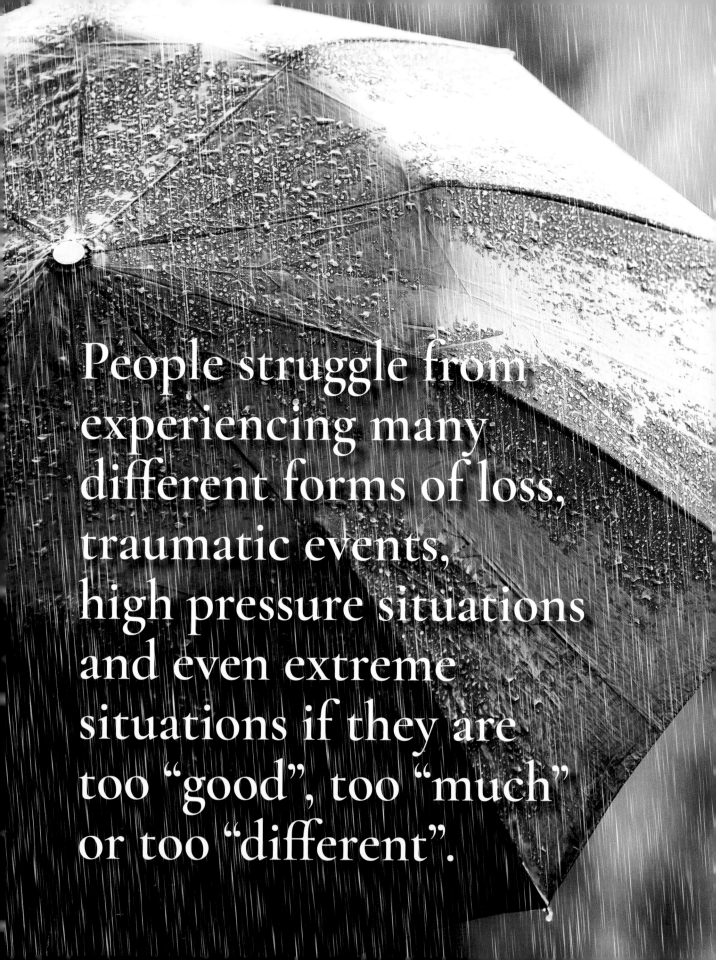

People struggle from experiencing many different forms of loss, traumatic events, high pressure situations and even extreme situations if they are too "good", too "much" or too "different".

THE NEED FOR COMFORT IS ALL AROUND US

Death
Loved one
Spouse
Parent
Child
Pet
Miscarriage/Stillbirth

Financial & Daily Needs
Money burdens and pressures
Job/Career
Bankruptcy

Physical Health
Hospitalization
Terminal Illness
Injury
Severe Injury/loss of mobilization
Homebound/Institutionalized
Special needs – person/parents/loved ones
Loss of function – hearing, seeing, ambulatory
Bed Ridden Pregnancies

Mental Health
Anxiety
Depression
Self-Harm
Obsessive-compulsive disorder
Addictions
Mood disorders
Eating disorders

Destruction of Property
Natural Disasters – Hurricane/Tornado/
Flood/Earthquake
House/Car/Business
Fire

Dissolution of purpose/work/dreams
Loss of job
Failed business proposal/plan
Unemployed
Job in crisis (downsizing, failed business)

Relationship Crisis
Severe conflict with others
Divorce/infidelity/breakup
Rebellious Teen and Adult children
Parenting Crisis
Family member in prison
Unwanted Pregnancy
Families separated due to work

Caregiving
Children with disabilites
Parents with memory loss or illness
Terminally ill family member
Spouse with severe illness
Children with illness or addictions

Lifestyle Changes
Caregiving roles
Religion
Gender
Sexuality
Living Location
Empty Nesters
Moving
Adoption
Foster

Extreme Concerns
Legal action
Financial pressures
Medical Tests
Impending layoffs
Rumors
Homelessness

Those Who Endure Hardship Serving Others
Doctors
Nurses
Clergy
Hospice Staff
Social Workers
Mental health professionals
Teachers
First Responders/Crisis and Disaster Response
Fire
Police
Veterans and Families

Trauma Conditions
Crisis Recovery
PTSD

Extreme Hopelessness
Bullying
Extreme Stress
Discouragement/Loss of Hope/Sadness/Rejection/Unforgiveness
Hidden Hurts

MACRO STRESSORS:
LIFE CHANGES

It's not just negative change that can cause high levels of stress. Any major change can create anxiety. Seemingly happy, yet big, changes such as getting married, having a baby, or moving for a new exciting job can make one feel as though they are living in an unfamiliar world. I know. I've been there.

The anxiety kept showing up. While driving, flying, in an elevator or even sitting with a group of people where I had to listen and not participate. I felt trapped and claustrophobic. All I could think was, "What is happening to me?". It was 1995 and I was in the middle of a 6 month battle with crippling anxiety.

Here's one example of what it was like – I remember sitting at a Broadway show in the middle of a super long row of seats (one of those rows where if you need to get up for any reason you need to walk past 30 very annoyed people) when I suddenly had this feeling that I had to get out. I couldn't concentrate on the show, my heart was racing and my hands started to shake. I felt trapped and thought I was losing my mind. I made it to intermission and left. No way was I going back in for the second half of the show. What had just happened?

A few months earlier I had returned to the US. Having wrapped up a job assignment in the Netherlands, I was coming home to get married. My fiancé at the time, and now husband, David had handled all the details for our new lives while I was working 3000 miles away. Upon returning from our honeymoon, I walked into a whole new reality. I was handed keys to a new car that I didn't pick out and drove up to a condo that I had not seen. Even though I was working for the same company, I began a new job with people who didn't know me, while adjusting to a very new pace of life, the New York way. Oh, by the way – welcome to married life!

On the outside, life was good. After all I had a great job with a great company and married an amazing man. How could I possibly be feeling anything less than elated? But inside, I was not myself. It took years to understand the reasons for the depth of my anxiety at that time. But there are reasons, which are illustrated in the Dr Rahe Life Change Stress Test shown here. In this test, a numerical value is given to different changes in life that can occur. And they can accumulate quickly if you have periods of massive change like I had. In this case, I was living with a score of 319 in Dr Rahe's life changes stress test. To put it in perspective, the death of a parent has a score of 100.

DR RAHE'S LIFE CHANGES STRESS TEST
THE "PILING ON" EFFECT

Use this scale as a simple guide to identify how much someone might need your support. (NOTE: While higher scores suggest that a person is more likely to need comfort or professional help, everyone is different and for the purpose of this book, these results are not a precise measurement.)

LOSS

Death of a spouse	119
Death of child	123
Death of brother or sister	102
Death of parent	100
Death of a close friend	70
Miscarriage or abortion	65

PHYSICAL HEALTH

An Injury or illness which: kept you in bed a week or more or sent you to the hospital	74
was less serious than above	44
Major change in health or behavior of family member	55
An accident	48
Major Dental Work	26
Major change in eating habits	27
Major change in sleeping habits	26
Major change in your usual type and/or amount of recreation	28

FINANCIAL

Major change in finances:	
Increased income	38
Decreased income	60
Investment and/or credit difficulties	56
Loss or damage of personal property	43
Moderate purchase	20
Major Purchase	37
Forclosure on a mortgage or loan	58

RELATIONSHIPS

Marriage	50
Divorce	96
New, close, personal relationship	37
Engaged to be married	45
Girlfriend or boyfriend problems	39
Falling out of a close personal relationships	47
Sexual difficulties	44
Separation from a spouse	
Due to work	28
Due to marital problems	76
Change in arguments with spouse	50

HOME & FAMILY

Major change in living conditions	42
Change in residence:	
Move within the same town or city	25
Move to a different town, city or state	47
Change in family get togethers	25
Pregnancy	67
Gain a new family member	
Birth of a child	66
Adoption of a child	65
A relative moving in with your	59
Child leaving home	41
To attend college	41
Due to marriage	45
For other reasons	
In-law problems	38
Change in the marital status of of your parents	
Divorce	58
Remarriage	50
Birth of a grandchild	43

WORK

Change to a new type of work	51
Change in work hours or conditions	35
Change in work responsibilites	
More responsibilities	29
Fewer responsibilities	21
Promotion	31
Demotion	42
Transfer	32
Spouse beginning or ending work	46
Troubles at work	
with your boss	29
with your coworkers	35
with persons under your supervision	35
Other work troubles	28
Major business adjustments	60
Retirement	52
Loss of Job	
Laid off from work	68
Fired from work	79

PERSONAL & SOCIAL

Change in personal habits	26
Beginning or ending school or college	38
Change of school or college	35
Change in political beliefs	24
Change in religious beliefs	29
Change in social activities	27
Minor violation of the law	20
Being held in jail	75
Major decision regarding your immediate future	51

Reprinted from the Journal of Psychosomatic Research, Life Changes scaling for the 1990s, Mark A. Miller, Richard H. Rahe Sep 1, 1997, Volume 43, Issue 3, pages 279-292, with permission from Elsevier.

MICRO STRESSORS:
LIFE CHANGES

The Rahe Scale is 24 years old but the stresses of life with our technology-laden, fast paced life are even more complex. In a Psychology Today article, Dr. Jasmin Tahmaseb-McConatha writes about a new concept that she calls microstressors. "Something is considered stressful when the demands of a task exceed our capacities" she says and continues, "The stressors we experience can generally be divided into two categories—day-to-day stressors and major life stressors. The great majority develop from daily occurrences—losing keys, sitting in traffic, running errands, being late, missing a meeting, etc. Any one of these, of course, is not as important as a major life event, such as marriage, illness, or retirement."

> "I need to access my bank account but I can't remember my password or where I wrote it down."

So when we are looking at someone needing comfort and support, major life changes and the Rahe scale don't adequately cover it anymore. We also need to consider the accumulation of the "little things".

3 out of 5 millennials recently answering a micro stressor survey believe that life is more stressful now than ever before because of these daily micro-stressors that previous generations did not experience.

Here are the top 20 micro-stressor scenarios reported by millennials:
1. Losing wallet/credit card
2. Arguing with partner
3. Commute/traffic delays
4. Losing phone
5. Arriving late to work
6. Slow WiFi
7. Phone battery dying
8. Forgetting passwords
9. Credit card fraud
10. Forgetting phone charger
11. Losing/misplacing keys
12. Paying bills
13. Job interviews
14. Phone screen breaking
15. Credit card bills
16. Check engine light coming on
17. School loan payments
18. Job security
19. Choosing what to wear
20. Washing dishes

Tahmaseb-McConatha adds a few more examples:

How can I open this package of chips? Where is the little tear sign?

Why does the water bottle cut my finger every time I try to open it?

How do I read my phone bill once I figure out what I am paying for?

Why do I have to wait 10 minutes to talk to a "satisfaction representative" when the company has made a mistake and overcharged me?

These micro stressors exemplify how our times have changed. No age group is escaping the accumulation of these. The actual micro stressors might change by your age, but I think most all of us will agree with the 30% of those surveyed that slow WiFi can sometimes be even more stressful than slow traffic.

If you add these to the major life changes that the Rahe Stress test demonstrates, you can begin to really paint the whole picture of how anxiety ridden our world is becoming, and how the accumulation of seemingly little things can be overwhelming.

Although these trends are troubling, we can also see how human connection and support can be a good remedy for these daily annoyances. Working through some of the stress and frustrations with a trusted friend or colleague can not only alleviate some of the stress but also strengthen a relationship. Recognizing that helping someone work through the simple problem of a broken phone screen could be the one thing to turn their day around.

Which in turn will make a real difference in our own lives.

WHAT I LEARNED GROWING UP IN THE AGE OF STRESS

BY KELLY SHANNON

I was born in 1996 – raised by Baby Boomers, and sandwiched between the generations that are considered "Millenials" and "Gen Z." I grew up occupying this liminal space between generations, and I feel as if I aged alongside certain technological advancements. The world shifted, and quickly.

Changes in culture and technology have certainly added a number of micro-stressors to our lives. There is pressure to maintain the perfect image of oneself, when all we see are curated versions of other people's lives online. And yes, we are a little bit addicted to technology.

As a member of the LGBTQ+ community who has struggled with mental health since I was seven, I was privileged to grow up in a well-off suburban neighborhood, which offered me so many opportunities in my life that I am grateful for – but also offered a good deal of challenges. I struggled with being bullied, as do so many kids in high school, and was ostracized for being gay before I was even out of the closet. And on top of this, I was – and continue to be - adjusting to and managing all these micro-stressors that result from a faster pace of life: from losing my schoolwork when my computer dies to figuring out how to pay credit card bills and student loans.

Because all these changes and advancements happened so quickly, we are learning to find a new balance between online and face-to-face interaction. We have new problems, new issues, and new ways of communicating. What we all need are resources for comfort. We need resources that show us new ways of connecting with one another when so much has changed.

Kelly Shannon is a performance artist, writer, researcher, and activist based in Connecticut. She is passionate about using somatics, performance, and movement to connect human beings to one another.

THINKING DIFFERENTLY
THE NEED FOR COMFORT NEVER ENDS

"When a person experiences a disruption in her life, you are needed. If you or other friends aren't available, the only person she has to talk with for guidance, support and direction is herself."
-H. NORMAN WRIGHT

I remember when I was in 7th grade and I was invited to be a guest in a concert band for a special performance. I went to a different school so knew no one in the band. I practiced and practiced and practiced, picked out my best outfit to wear, and tried my best not to feel awkward as I took to the stage with people I didn't know. Before the concert started, the conductor asked the entire band to stand up and one by one each participant was given a recognition certificate for their achievement. Because I was from a different school my name was left off the list. And so I was left standing alone after all the certificates were handed out and the conductor moved on with getting the concert underway. I slowly sat down knowing every single eye in that auditorium was wondering why I was left standing alone and didn't get recognized. It's always stayed with me.

I have listened to hundreds of people talk about losses, crisis and trauma. Many from years and years ago. And as I listened, I was left wondering, "If I can still recall with vivid detail that silly band concert from over 40 years ago, imagine how vivid and traumatic the memories are of those who

have faced unimaginable loss and tragedy, regardless of how many years ago it was". If we can remember our most embarrassing moments in life and recall them with exceptional clarity, why would we expect anyone to forget the pain of tremendous loss, crisis or trauma any faster?

All the major events that happen in our lives change us. It's just the way life works. Life never goes back to its old course. The map changes. So then it's important that we honor these major life events and acknowledge them. That we learn to see the new person emerging instead of ignoring the change. That we are there to chart a new course with each other.

I'm suggesting we flip our lenses and change our perspective. Diving into someones pain with them will help them and help you. You will have a deeper bond and a more trusting relationship because you cared and pushed through the awkward.

This doesn't have to be hard. We can learn that life will blend together the past, present and future. That each and every part of our lives make us who we are.

So, let's change our perspective.

AVOID THE 10 PITFALLS OF COMFORTING

These may be some of the most important tidbits
in this book for you to remember.

PLEASE DON'T ASSUME THAT		WHY
They are "over it" have "moved on" or should be over it or should move on.	1	People never "get over" trauma and loss. Each and every change in our lives deepens our character and makes us who we are. They are on a whole new journey.
You know how they feel.	2	Comparison is the great uncomforter. Pain and loss are like fingerprints. No two are the same. Peoples response to the same or a similar situation can be dramatically different.
Giving them "some space" is a good thing.	3	Space grows isolation & loneliness. Unless they ask for it, don't assume they want it.
Giving them advice will help them.	4	Advice is the big no no. Please don't go there unless they ask you for it.
Cheering them up is what they need.	5	Changing the mood will put up a wall between you. Being present with someone and validating what they are experiencing is most helpful.
They are exaggerating their struggle or making it up for attention.	6	Their struggle is real to them.
If you bring up the struggle it will upset them.	7	Many times it's because people DON'T bring up the struggle that people feel isolated.
There is a set timeframe for healing, and they are abiding to that.	8	There. Is. No. Set. Timeframe. For. Healing. End. Of. Story.
Saying the name of someone who passed will make them upset.	9	Those who have experienced the death of someone close to them don't want that person to be forgotten. They want to preserve the memories they shared with them.
They can replace a loss to help relieve their pain. (ie have another baby, get another dog, etc...)	10	There is no "new" anything that will take the place of a loss. This can be seen as very dismissive and hurtful.

SUPPORT IS A LONG TERM ENDEAVOR

When a tragic event happens, there is a general way that the support occurs. It is heavily loaded in the beginning or soon after the event happens. It tapers off to a slow trickle of support sooner than most people realize. When we take time to recognize this, it takes the pressure off of doing the one perfect thing right at the beginning of the cycle. Care and support are usually appreciated the most after everyone else has forgotten and moved on.

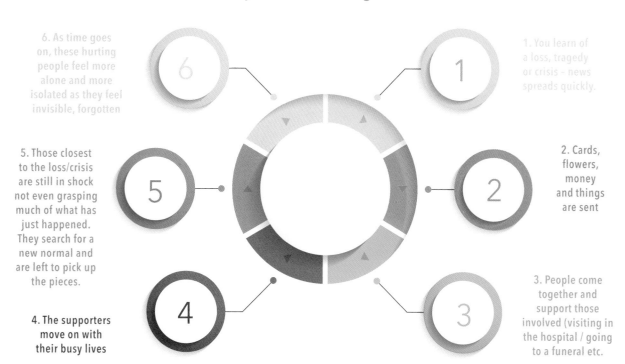

6. As time goes on, these hurting people feel more alone and more isolated as they feel invisible, forgotten

1. You learn of a loss, tragedy or crisis – news spreads quickly.

5. Those closest to the loss/crisis are still in shock not even grasping much of what has just happened. They search for a new normal and are left to pick up the pieces.

2. Cards, flowers, money and things are sent

4. The supporters move on with their busy lives

3. People come together and support those involved (visiting in the hospital / going to a funeral etc.

IT'S ALWAYS WITH YOU: When we remove "getting over it", "moving on" and "getting back to normal" from our thought process and replace our thinking with "it's always with you", we change everything.

"Getting over it" puts up a big dark wall, denying most reflection and conversation on the topic; **"always with you"** breaks that wall down and opens a beautiful door for preserving memories, accepting & providing comfort and building relationships based on the memories and pain.

"Moving on" discourages looking back, marching blindly forward; **"always with you"** takes the past and seamlessly weaves it into the present and future. Using each day, the bad days with the good days, to bring together the full story.

"Getting back to normal" is sometimes mistaken for finding a way to go on; **"always with you"** allows for true resiliency by identifying and accepting a "new normal" and living life as it is now.

HOPE FROM AN UNTHINKABLE TRAGEDY:
CRAIG GREENLEE'S REFLECTIONS 49 YEARS LATER

Craig Greenlee is the author of the book *November Ever After: A Memoir of Tragedy and Triumph in the Wake of the 1970 Marshall Football Plane Crash* in which he chronicles the trauma of losing dozens of his college football teammates and coaches in a plane crash. He waited 40 years to tell his story. He knew most of those who were on the plane that night. He was on the team the previous two seasons, left the team for personal reasons and came back for spring practice in 1971 to help rebuild the football program.

Craig has a southern drawl and deep commitment to preserve the memories of his beloved teammates and all those affected by this tragedy. Craig reflected with me on the struggle of living in a world where no one could possibly understand what you were going through. How could anyone possibly understand? Wanting to be strong, but not sure of the path forward.

There was no roadmap and so, he learned as he went on.

49 years later, here are some wise takeaways from Craig for those of needing comfort or for those attempting to comfort others:

WHAT HE LEARNED:

We need each other more than we want to admit.

"You help yourself helping yourself. Don't underestimate your emotion. Don't think "I'll get over it". Seek help. Find people you trust and open up.

Helping others helped us.

Joe Bundy was a freshman student who was assigned to assist the father of one of the players who died. In the book, Bundy recalled "Rather than thinking about how bad I felt about losing a homeboy, my focus changed. I began to think about what it must be like for the parent in the situation. It allowed me to be strong.".

Everyone will respond differently.

A loss of any kind is a matter of the heart. It's something we all have to understand because we will all deal with it at some point in our lives. And how people respond to crisis, trauma and loss are as different as our fingerprints." You can have no expectation of how people are dealing with their trauma other than they have not forgotten it.

Memories of the event don't fade to black. When we think about the fact that we still have vivid memories from our childhood, how could we expect that those suffering from trauma don't have flashbacks of what they experienced with exceptional clarity? Craig recalls his memories like he's watching them on film. They are that clear to him.

WHAT OTHERS COULD LEARN

Be patient

"When you are so deep in pain there simply are no words. Don't expect people to open up and talk about it. Be patient. We consoled each other in silence. The pain was so profound. "

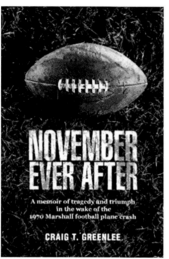

"When you are so deep in pain there simply are no words. Don't expect people to open up and talk about it. Be patient."

Be mindful of saying hurtful things.

Shocking things. Angry things. Clueless things. With so much pain around its unavoidable. Craig recalls vividly things said that were anything but helpful:

"It's about time that you move on from that plane crash"

"People die, and they're buried, and you just move on,"

Craig closes his book with this:

What we can say is that we endured. And during that process, we wept, and we agonized. And we continued to celebrate the lives of those who perished. The Marshall students from the early '70s are senior citizens now. We've established ourselves in our careers, raised our children and are having a ball as grandparents. Along the way, we've lost loved ones, which includes parents, siblings, other relatives and in some cases lifelong buddies. Even with all of that, we cannot erase the memories from over 40 years ago, memories that are forever etched in our psyches. True enough, it was so long ago, but it's still just like it happened yesterday. It's always with you"

THE POWERFUL FULL BODY EXPERIENCE OF GIVING COMFORT

It's so much more about the heart than it is the brain. The second we try to "solve" the situation, we fail. Because people who need comfort don't want solving. They want you.

I still cringe when I think of it. It was early in my comforting days and I was still a bit unaware of how to comfort correctly.

I was at a swim meet and a family who had recently lost a child was also there. I really didn't know them, but nonetheless decided to go "comfort them". Probably not the wisest of choices at a loud swim meet with parents yelling, kids running everywhere, whistles blowing and water splashing.

I went over to them thinking I was very brave and introduced myself and told them how sorry I was. I was totally 100% stuck in the awkward zone, speaking useless platitudes. There was no breaking through the awkward this time. I knew I wasn't helping but kept digging myself in. In looking back, I wish I would have been more aware of the whole body of comfort. I could have avoided that terribly uncomfortable exchange. I missed the point entirely.

In my haste to help, I was more focused on using my mouth to speak comfort than I was at using my eyes to really see this competitive and stressful environment and the distracting situations it created. I should have asked my heart to override my brain.

FULL BODY OF COMFORT

Why are we so focused on the mouth? In this case, to use the mouth to force conversation; or other times to use words as an excuse to avoid doing anything at all because we don't know what words to say? The mouth is such a tiny part of our body. That day at the pool taught me that I needed to use my mouth differently.

I started to remember that my brain could get in the way just as much as my mouth. As I look back on all of my years of providing and observing comfort, I've realized it's all about the heart. The second I try to engage my brain and try to "solve" the situation, I fail. Because people who need comfort don't want solving. They want you and your heart. They want to be cared for and loved. And love doesn't start with the brain, it's all heart. I think about the fact that if I would have gone to school to write this book, I would have been tripped up. Because I would have had to focus on my brain; on science and on data and on hypothesis and studies. And don't get me wrong, that's really important. But it has been the 7 years of using my heart that has given me the perspective and shown me the way. Now I'm able to apply the science to what my heart has learned.

It takes your full body to be the best comforter you can be. We have two eyes, two ears, two hands, two feet, two arms and two legs and ONE mouth. Use them accordingly to this proportion! It's actually comforting to take the pressure off the mouth, right? It's what usually trips us up.

COMFORT STARTS IN THE HEART

Impactful comforting doesn't come from the brain– it comes from our heart and body. Here's how to use our own tools to help comfort others.

USE YOUR
BRAIN
TO REMEMBER YOUR COMFORTING SKILLS

USE YOUR
FEET
TO SHOW UP

"To handle yourself, use your head; to handle others, use your heart."

–ELEANOR ROOSEVELT

HEART & BRAIN

No body part is more important in the comfort process than the heart. But in our screen to screen world, we use our brains so much more than our hearts, so this concept requires new perspective. When we grasp the difference between the function of the brain and the function of the heart, comforting becomes much easier.

BRAIN	HEART
Used for learning.	Used for caring.
Leads us to "fix it" mode.	Leads us to "love and understanding" mode.
Wants to know all the details.	Wants to know where it hurts the most.
Operates mostly in the "me" mode.	Operates in the "you" mode.
Leads to "comparative stories" and advice.	Wants to listen and help.
Listens with curiosity.	Listens in love.
Is "book smart".	Is "people smart".
Rules the busy world.	Works in the pausing and in the stillness.
Seeks to answer the *why.*	Seeks to answer the *how.*

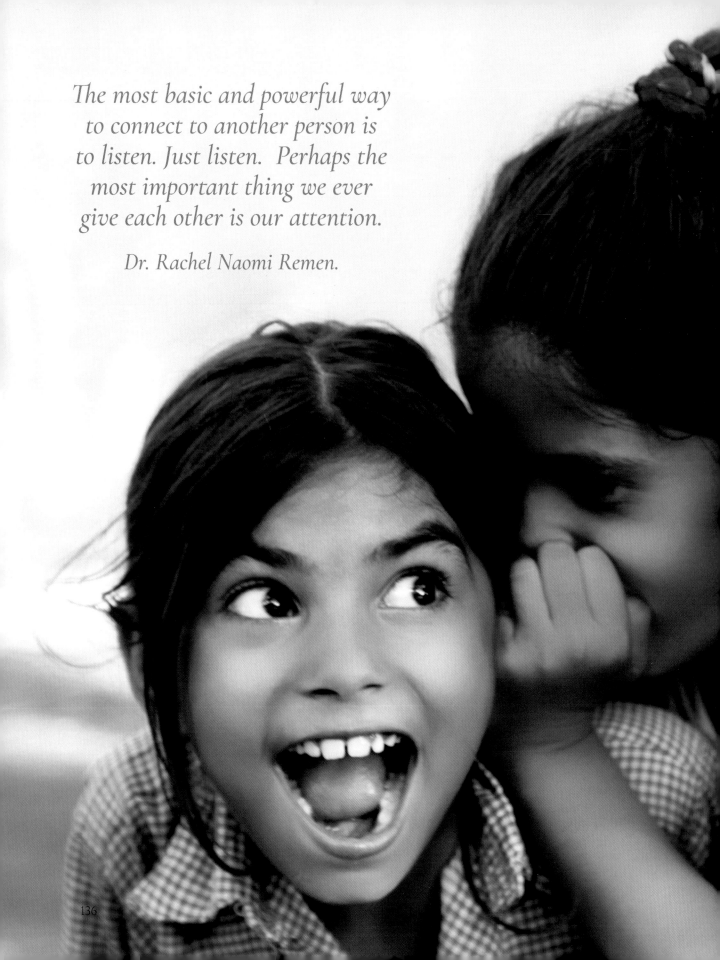

The most basic and powerful way to connect to another person is to listen. Just listen. Perhaps the most important thing we ever give each other is our attention.

Dr. Rachel Naomi Remen.

EARS

Like comfort, listening is a skill that can be learned. And like comfort, the key to the skill of listening is in the PAUSING. And there is something rather calming about that thought. You don't have to constantly think about what you're going to say next, you just need to be there. In our "Comfort Lab" with thousands of one-to-one connections, we have seen this time and time again. Being present and listening are the two most important things we can offer someone.

Relax and remember this isn't about you. It's all about the person that wants you there.

Listen to understand not to reply.

5 *GUIDELINES* WHEN LISTENING TO COMFORT:

1. Open your heart

Think about how you are caring for this person. Take a big breath and let your heart be prepared to connect. One heart to one heart.

2. Connect with them

Lean in to them, and if appropriate, touch their hand, connect with your eyes, force yourself to keep your eyes on them. Try not look away, even if they do.

3. Hear to understand

Look at them and really hear what they are saying. Attempt to understand what emotion or emotions they may be experiencing.

4. Allow silence

Although uncomfortable at times, silence allows for you to just be present and for the person to collect their thoughts, and reflect on how they are feeling at that specific moment allowing them to better assess their current emotions.

5. Listen to comfort

What are their needs?
What did you hear you could do?

" I realized John couldn't pay his rent with the medical bills piling up, maybe I could help?

"While listening to Sally, I realized I could pick up her kids once a week and give her time to herself."

"Hearing Judy talk about having to get home to her mother, I offered to stay late for her and complete the work project."

5 *PITFALLS* WHEN LISTENING TO COMFORT:

1. Busy

Although we recognize the pace of life is fast, comforting does mean to, at times put aside our own busyness, to Pause and stop to comfort one who needs us.

2. Bad timing

When someone needs you it might not be the most convenient time for you, but it is the time to assess how and when you can respond to them.

3. Too emotional

We are human and we cannot help feeling emotional while comforting someone, however focusing on their needs in the moment can help.

4. Electronics

The sound of a notification on your cell phone is distracting to say the least, good to double check your phone is off.

5. Trying to fix it

The second we try to give advice we turn off our listening ears and turn to a talking mouth. Remember, you are not responsible to fix, only to comfort.

> "The most important thing in communication is hearing what isn't said."
>
> *– PETER F. DRUCKER*

LISTENING BY THE NUMBERS

45%
Amount of time we spend listening

85%
Percentage of what we know we have learned by listening

30%
Reduction in office visits by chronically ill patients after they have been listened to for 15-30 min.

WHEN YOU TALK YOU ARE ONLY REPEATING WHAT YOU ALREADY KNOW, BUT IF YOU LISTEN YOU MAY LEARN SOMETHING NEW.

–DALAI LAMA.

20%
How much we remember of what we hear after 2-5 days

75%
Amount of the time we are distracted, preoccupied or forgetful when listening

50%
How much we usually recall immediately after we listen to someone talk

EYES

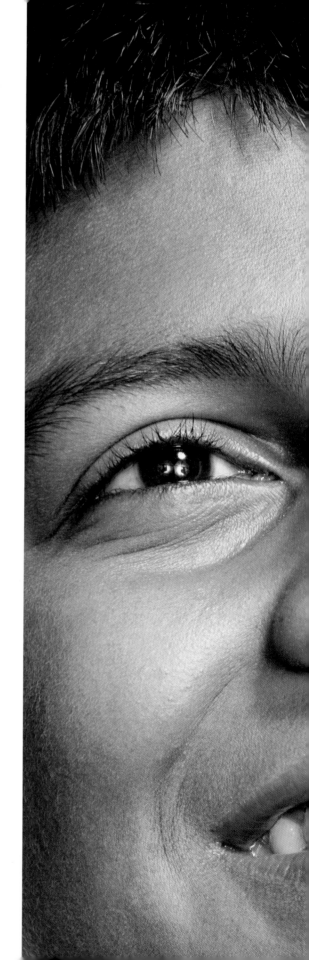

Dina walked into the bakery and stepped into line behind me. "Hi" she said. I turned and said "Oh hey Dina, how are you doing"? "I'm o.k", she said as she quickly turned her eyes away from me. I noticed a sad look to her face, and saw that her hair was messy and dirty which was not like her usual perfectly straight and clean hair. She stared out the window and tapped her foot as we waited to order almost as if she forgot I was there. My eyes saw past her words as I said, "I'm going to sit here with my coffee if you'd like to join me"? (I hadn't planned on doing that, but wanted to offer her the chance to talk.) "I'd like that" she answered.

When someone is in need of comfort, there are clues that we can see which alert us to this need. Our eyes can pick up on many subtle changes that can't be heard in words. It's often done instinctively rather than consciously. Our words communicate how we are feeling but our nonverbal cues sometimes speak the loudest.

Dr Albert Mehrabian is one of the leading researchers on non verbal communication. His Elements of Personal Communication chart on page 144 demonstrates just how important our eyes are in seeing what is being communicated. Gestures, posture, facial expression, eye contact – "eye talk"–things only our eyes can pick up on. Like Dina, we can say one thing, but our body language is saying something else.

Using our eyes to recognize who needs comfort, we can accurately be more aware of other people's emotions, including how they are feeling and the unspoken messages they're sending. Additionally we can create trust when we connect with them by sending them nonverbal signals that show that we understand and care.

"A person who truly cares is the one who sees the pain in your eyes while everyone else believes in the smile on your face."

—UNKNOWN

INVISIBLE WOUNDS

Sometimes no matter how carefully we look for those in need of comfort, there are often factors at work that we can't see with our eyes. Just because we don't see hardship, it doesn't mean that a person is without struggle. Listen to the voices of people who have experienced profound sadness, anxiety, depression, loneliness.

"I have this problem: I isolate myself, then become upset because I'm lonely."

-UNKNOWN

"It was against my principles and all, but I was feeling so depressed I didn't even think. That's the whole trouble. When you're feeling very depressed, you can't even think."

– J.D. SALINGER

"I knew a girl in high school that always complained about having anxiety. I used to make fun of her a little bit. It looked like nothing to me. So I assumed it was nothing. And I dealt with it by trying to convince her that it was nothing. I called her recently to apologize. I've had really bad anxiety ever since my father died. And it's definitely not nothing. It's the indescribable fear of nothing."

– HUMANS OF NEW YORK.

"I am exhausted from trying to be stronger than I feel."

-UNKNOWN

"It feels like everyone else is moving on with their lives while I am stuck here in this hole that I can't climb out of."
— UNKNOWN

"I know what it's like to be afraid of your own mind" -
DR. REID/CRIMINAL MINDS

"I don't think people understand how stressful it is to explain what's going on in your head when you don't even understand it yourself."
-Unknown

"EVERY MAN HAS HIS SECRET SORROWS WHICH THE WORLD KNOWS NOT; AND OFTEN TIMES WE CALL A MAN COLD WHEN HE IS ONLY SAD."
–HENRY WADSWORTH LONGFELLOW

"Everyone gets tired of me at some point. Then eventually they'll leave. They all do."
–Unknown

"Have you ever been so close to crying but you smile anyways?"
–UNKNOWN

"Confession: Sometimes I get anxious because I don't feel anxious. Which means I forgot what I was supposed to feel anxious about in the first place and that gives me anxiety."
-Unknown

AS WE USE OUR EYES TO COMFORT, LOOK FOR THESE SIGNALS:

- [ ] They've become withdrawn and don't get together or talk to you as often as they used to
- [ ] They don't seem "present" when you talk to them – their mind seems to be somewhere else.
- [ ] You notice they post their problems on social media
- [ ] Displays Increased use of alcohol and drugs and other high risk behaviors
- [ ] More negative emotions than normal – angry, grumpy, teary, goofy
- [ ] They can't relax and can be very jittery
- [ ] Not sleeping or Sleeping all the time
- [ ] Avoids all hobbies or things they used to enjoy
- [ ] Expresses "I'm actually scared. I feel like bad things are going to happen to me."
- [ ] Makes isolating statements such as "I make it very hard for people to help me when all I want to do is be left alone"
- [ ] Describes their day - "I can get through the day if I avoid any interaction with people. I will keep my head down and avoid any situation where I have to interact with another human being."
- [ ] Experiences a Change in Eating habits - either eating way more or way less than they used to
- [ ] It's hard for them to concentrate, almost like a "Fog" - they can often repeat what they've said many times, or lose a train of thought and never finish the sentence.
- [ ] Simple tasks that used to be easy become extremely hard to focus on. Examples are laundry or grocery shopping or paying bills.
- [ ] Feels physical pain – "my skin hurts, my teeth hurt, my hair hurts

- [ ] Has a sense of Apathy
- [ ] Is Exhausted
- [ ] Acts Stressed
- [ ] Appears Disorganized
- [ ] Describes a sense of Desperation
- [ ] Rapid Change of emotions - anger / sadness / despair / hope
- [ ] Feels like no one can relate
- [ ] Feels like they are broken and everyone around them is whole
- [ ] Describes Feeling like the world is going 500 miles an hour and they are sitting still.
- [ ] Describes feeling Helpless and alone
- [ ] Cancels last minute plans
- [ ] Obsess over cleaning or other details
- [ ] Over-plan everything
- [ ] Pick their skin, or their nails
- [ ] Change driving habits to avoid busy roads or congestion
- [ ] Will turn down plans to go to concerts or travel to avoid crowds
- [ ] Nervous body habits like shaking a leg or tapping a pencil
- [ ] Friend circle changes or disappears entirely.
- [ ] Family dynamic/life changes.
- [ ] Financial status changes.
- [ ] Job situation changes.
- [ ] It effects self worth, self esteem, confidence
- [ ] Sense of security, sense of humor and sense of self

OUR EYES MAY SEE A NEED BEFORE OUR EARS HEAR ONE

When we are looking for signs of distress, there are even more things that you can watch for outside of daily conversation that will allow you to help even more.

IN CONVERSATION

- ☐ Eye Contact – is the person making consistent eye contact with you or are their eyes darting, staring in the distance or looking down?
- ☐ Facial Expressions – are they unexpressive, sad, or angry?
- ☐ Appearance – Has there been a change in their clothing or weight?
- ☐ Posture – relaxed or stressed
- ☐ Body gestures – hands and arm movements
- ☐ Proximity – are they close or distant
- ☐ Distracted and antsy – Leg's swinging/Finger tapping / clenched fists – indications of stress
- ☐ Tears / Eyes watering – expressing emotion

OUTSIDE OF CONVERSATION

- ☐ Schedule – Their normal routine has dramatically changed
- ☐ Diet – are they eating or drinking differently
- ☐ Engagement – are they less engaged with friend groups
- ☐ Events – do they make plans and then cancel

ELEMENTS OF PERSONAL COMMUNICATION

7% spoken words
38% voice, tone
55% body language

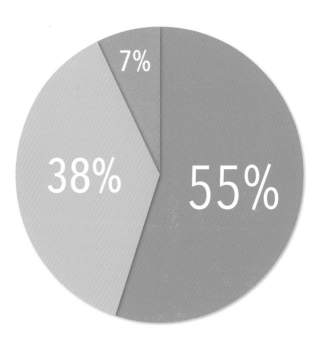

SIGNS OF SUICIDAL BEHAVIOR

WHAT LEADS TO SUICIDE?

There's no single cause for suicide. Suicide most often occurs when stressors and health issues converge to create an experience of hopelessness and despair. Depression is the most common condition associated with suicide, and it is often undiagnosed or untreated. Conditions like depression, anxiety and substance problems, especially when unaddressed, increase risk for suicide. Yet it's important to note that most people who actively manage their mental health conditions go on to engage in life.

SUICIDE WARNING SIGNS

Something to look out for when concerned that a person may be suicidal is a change in behavior or the presence of entirely new behaviors. This is of sharpest concern if the new or changed behavior is related to a painful event, loss, or change. Most people who take their lives exhibit one or more warning signs, either through what they say or what they do.

 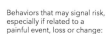    

Talk

If a person talks about:

- Killing themselves
- Feeling hopeless
- Having no reason to live
- Being a burden to others
- Feeling trapped
- Unbearable pain

Behavior

Behaviors that may signal risk, especially if related to a painful event, loss or change:

- Increased use of alcohol or drugs
- Looking for a way to end their lives, such as searching online for methods
- Withdrawing from activities
- Isolating from family and friends
- Sleeping too much or too little
- Visiting or calling people to say goodbye
- Giving away prized possessions
- Aggression
- Fatigue

Mood

People who are considering suicide often display one or more of the following moods:

- Depression
- Anxiety
- Loss of interest
- Irritability
- Humiliation/Shame
- Agitation/Anger
- Relief/Sudden Improvement

Health Factors

- Mental health conditions
  - Depression
  - Substance use problems
  - Bipolar disorder
  - Schizophrenia
  - Personality traits of aggression, mood changes and poor relationships
  - Conduct disorder
  - Anxiety disorders
- Serious physical health conditions including pain
- Traumatic brain injury

Environmental Factors

- Access to lethal means including firearms and drugs
- Prolonged stress, such as harassment, bullying, relationship problems or unemployment
- Stressful life events, like rejection, divorce, financial crisis, other life transitions or loss
- Exposure to another person's suicide, or to graphic or sensationalized accounts of suicide

Historical Factors

- Previous suicide attempts
- Family history of suicide
- Childhood abuse, neglect or trauma

Thank you to AFSP for this information

147

MOUTH

I recently moved to Virginia from Connecticut where we had lived for over 12 years. The 12 main family years. You know those years - school, sports, dances, band concerts, confirmations, graduations and birthday parties. All the laughs and tears and friends and activities that had become such an integral part of my life were about to be left behind.

The thought of moving out of one house and moving into another one, coupled with starting fresh with everything was exhausting. My husband had a new job, two of my girls were off to college and my youngest daughter was starting High School. It seemed that everyone was set with their path ahead but me. Nothing was physically wrong, but my heart was broken.

My family & friends know that I love to talk. A lot. I love to laugh and hang out with friends. I am not shy, and I love people. So, it's really easy to see how some did not take me seriously when I told them how much I didn't want to move. How tough it was going to be. Or maybe they did but didn't know what to say, because we all know that happens too. And what was the line I heard the most? What was the line I wanted to scream every single time I heard it?

"You're going to be fine." Or "You'll do great." Or "You'll make friends in no time."

I really wanted to scream each and every time I heard these terrible horrible no good very bad lines. Shake the poor friend of mine and say "I KNOW I'LL BE FINE! BUT THAT'S NOT WHAT I WANT TO HEAR". I just wanted people to say "I know it sucks right? I'm so sorry. You know I'll always be here. I'm going to miss you." That's all. I just wanted people to hug me and say it was all going to be ok.

Dr. Kenneth C Hauk, in his great book, "Don't Sing Songs to a Heavy Heart" calls these kind of phrases "Pink Thinking". Pink thinking behaviors gloss over, deny or minimize the painful reality of a suffering person. And it's easy to see why we say these phrases, because face it, we all do. We say these kinds of things because we want the person to know how much we believe in them. Our initial instinct is to solve their hurt. Not be in their hurt with them.

Knowing how and when to use our mouths will make these situations way easier.

> Sometimes no words are the best words of all. Silence can never be misquoted

To comfort, one must be comfortable being uncomfortable.

WHAT TO SAY AND HOW TO SAY IT

When you are preparing to comfort someone in person, consider your mouth first. Your words have the power to completely set the tone.

1. Facial Expression - Your mouth (along with your eyes) are key players in your your facial expression, which is critical if you are interacting with someone face to face. Turn those lips up, even if it's an incredibly sad occasion. Always be happy to see them.

2. Talking - To talk or not to talk, this is the question. Think back to the lessons we learn from dogs. They can't talk, and yet they are comfort machines. We can do that too– and avoid awkward exchanges in the future– by realizing that talking is actually one of the least important aspects of comforting. Keep this in mind as we move forward to "what we can say" and "what we can do" in the pages ahead.

BEFORE YOU SPEAK, TAKE A MOMENT TO CHECK IF YOUR WORDS PASS THE *P.A.U.S.E.* COMFORT FILTER TEST:

PATIENCE - Is it the right time to be saying these words? Are you talking just to fill the silence?

ADVICE - Are you trying to give advice when someone didn't ask for a solution?

UNLOADING - Are you unloading your own thoughts & experiences onto this person instead of listening?

STAY - Are you staying with the person's mood, or are you trying to change it?

EMPHASIS - Is the emphasis of the conversation on them, or on you?

SIX THINGS TO CONSIDER BEFORE YOU SPEAK:

1. Put your phone away

Don't let electronic distractions interfere with your conversation.

2. Lead with your heart

To touch another's heart, your words need to originate from your own heart. You need to simply care for this person. Nothing more nothing less.

3. Are words even needed?

Sometimes there are no words. Don't force them. Just be there.

4. Consider an action instead of words.

Sometimes people who are hurting prefer not to talk but desperately want to know that you care. Look at pages 172 -186 for ideas.

5. Respect the silent pauses

and allow time for each of you to formulate the right words. Watch the non verbal cues in those silences to guide you and don't break the silence just because it's uncomfortable.

6. It's all worth it - Stick with it!

Relationships grow very deep when we don't give up on each other. We work through the peaks and valleys together. We support each other in the good times and bad even though it's awkward and hard and we feel like we would rather be doing something else.

WHEN WE DO OPEN OUR MOUTHS

"Speak in a way that others love to listen to you and listen in a way that others love to speak to you."

One of the greatest conversation stoppers to those who need comfort is when we move the source of conversation away from the one needing support and on to ourselves. We all do it. Sociologist Charles Derber calls this "Conversational Narcissism" in his influential study The Pursuit of Attention.

It happens without us even knowing it, because its human nature to want to talk about ourselves. Especially with comforting it will take being aware of this secret shift to keep the focus on the one who needs you.

These simple examples show how this works. The shift response versus the support response. When we keep the conversation off of us and focus on the person we are supporting, it's amazing how much insight we will gain and how much easier it will be to comfort.

A FEW EXAMPLES OF SHIFT RESPONSE VS SUPPORT RESPONSE

Example #1

John: I'm feeling really overwhelmed.
Mary: I know, I'm so busy too!
(shift-response)

John: I'm feeling really overwhelmed.
Mary: Tell me what's going on?
(support-response)

Example #2

John: I didn't get any sleep, my mom's Alzheimer's is getting worse.
Mary: I'm sorry, my neighbor's mom has Alzheimer's too.
(shift-response)

John: I didn't get any sleep, my mom's Alzheimer's is getting worse.
Mary: You must so tired, would you like to talk about it?
(support-response)

"I HAVE NO IDEA WHAT TO SAY"

No one escapes the dreaded awkwardness of not knowing what to say. Awkwardness doesn't discriminate. It doesn't matter if you are an introvert or an extrovert, rich or poor, happy or sad, black or white, young or old. But it really doesn't have to be this way.

We've heard from hundreds of people over the years as to what were the best or worst things people said or did. What we are learning is that most times things fail when they are forced. So take a deep breath, pause and let's tackle this awkwardness with words!

When I was fighting cancer, the little greeting cards of encouragement and small tokens came from some that I hardly knew. I saved each and every card I received during that journey. Some friends that I was quite close to I had to keep at a distance, as I realized they were draining me of my emotional energy with their own drama. I hadn't realized before my own illness and the kindness I had received that a few of my friendships were one sided, with my giving support the majority of time. The generosity and support of other friends really helped me discover friendship could be a 2 way street and that I was deserving of that love.

I invited a friend, a mom who lost her young daughter to suicide, to a pool party and while we visited and her son swam, she told me that everyone else treated her differently now and was afraid to talk to her. I just followed her lead and we talked about makeup, fashion, kids, school. When we parted I hugged her tight and she said "keep inviting us?"

I didn't usually seek comfort from others but have started to realize how critical it is for my wellbeing. It had been a rough year for me. We were having our annual extended family summer crab boil and my 18 year old son would not be there this year for the first time. He was in a full time treatment program for some mental health issues which everyone was aware of. My sister in law called to discuss the party and I have to say I was shocked and saddened as she complained to me about everything under the sun regarding her own children. A full 30 minutes into our conversation she never once asked how I was doing. How I felt about having one of my kids absent from the annual event. She just dumped on me and went on and on about her kids, completely insensitive to what I was going through and how this party might be difficult on me. Her negative energy and lack of concern drained me. If only she had slowed down to think, she may have had time to actually say " I know this will be difficult for you is there anything I can do." I really didn't need much at that moment - just a little recognition of the situation.

A good friend of mine lost her dad some years back. I found her sitting alone outside our workplace, just staring at the horizon. She was absolutely distraught, and I didn't know what to say to her. It's so easy to say the wrong thing to someone who is grieving and vulnerable.

So I started talking about how I grew up without a father. I told her my dad had drowned in a submarine when I was only nine months old and I'd always mourned his loss, even though I'd never known him. I wanted her to realize that she wasn't alone, that I'd been through something similar and I could understand how she felt.

But after I related this story, my friend snapped, "Okay, Celeste, you win. You never had a dad and I at least got to spend 30 years with mine. You had it worse. I guess I shouldn't be so upset that my dad just died."

I was stunned and mortified. "No, no, no," I said, "that's not what I'm saying at all. I just meant I know how you feel." And she answered, "No, Celeste, you don't. You have no idea how I feel."

She walked away and I stood there feeling like a jerk. I had wanted to comfort her and, instead, I'd made her feel worse. When she began to share her raw emotions, I felt uncomfortable so I defaulted to a subject with which I was comfortable: myself. She wanted to talk about her father, to tell me about the kind of man he was. She wanted to share her cherished memories. Instead, I asked her to listen to my story.

Celeste Headlee, TED Guest Author

My husband was transferred to a hospital in Newark in the middle of the night (3am) in kidney and liver failure and I was overwhelmed. At 6am I headed to the cafeteria and got coffee and was looking for one of those cardboard carriers and as I was aimlessly wandering the cafeteria a worker came over and asked if I was OK. I must have looked awful and confused, I made a gesture with my hand what I was looking for. "She asked why I was there." I had barely explained my husband's situation when she touched my shoulder and said "Don't worry sista we may be in da hood but we good" and lifted her shirt to show two different scars and explained the she had a liver and kidney transplant and this was the best place to be! At that moment it was exactly what I needed to comfort me and help ease my mind. She "saw" me and knew what I needed at the time. I think we need to "see" people and understand the smallest gesture can make a difference.

WORDS AND PHRASES THAT CAN BE HURTFUL

- "Why" questions. Avoid them all.
- Are you okay?
- I know just how you feel.
- How are you? How are you doing?
- Please let me know....
- Be sure to take care of yourself
- Any advice of any kind... just don't go there
- I'll pray for you (when you say it just to say it)
- Don't forget to take care of yourself
- Just hang in there
- Promising something that you don't follow through on / Making promises you can't keep
- Talking just to fill the silence
- This will make your family stronger
- Next time we will be sure not to use that doctor or hospital
- Be Brave
- Get ahold of yourself
- I think you're in denial
- It's better to have loved and lost than never to have loved
- Big boys don't cry, suck it up
- Time heals everything
- AT LEAST... ANYTHING... don't ever ever say AT LEAST
- You Should, or You Shouldn't... anything... advice is bad
- I know how you feel (you don't)
- It's for the best
- Isn't it time to move on with your life?
- It's God's will
- It was his/her time to go
- God wanted another angel
- Come on, it's not so bad.
- There is always someone who has it worse than you
- You should put this all behind you and enjoy the life you have ahead
- He/She's in a better place
- It was just....
- Just hang in there
- Time will heal everything
- You have to be strong for.....
- Look on the bright side
- At least you have more children, be glad it wasn't your only child
- God doesn't give you more than you can handle
- You weren't really that close to your stepmother anyway, right?
- COMPARISON of any kind! Please don't try to compare their situation to anything you have experienced or heard of
- You're young...
- What doesn't kill you makes you stronger
- If only you would have done ___ this might not have happened.
- You'll meet someone new (if you've lost a significant other)
- It must have been Gods plan / will
- No dwelling on the past.
- When are you going to get over this?
- You need to take better care of yourself
- All of that is in the past now
- Everyone dies sooner or later, right?
- It's been 3 months, you should be getting back to normal now?
- You should be joyful even when times are hard
- I don't understand why you are still sad after all this time. Life needs to go on.

WORDS THAT *UN*COMFORT ME

DON'T UNCOMFORT ME!

There is a time and place for motivating me and encouraging me on. But when I am down and struggling please don't try to tell me to look on the bright side and how strong I am!

☐ You're going to get through this! You're so strong.
☐ You'll be fine!
☐ You'll do great!
☐ You'll be back on your feet in no time.
☐ Don't worry, you'll be better soon!
☐ Look on the bright side...
☐ You're so outgoing, you'll make lots of new friends to fill the void.
☐ You'll get over this in no time.
☐ I know that whatever happens, you'll do fine. I have faith in you!
☐ You can start a whole new life now!
☐ It's a beautiful day outside, put a smile on your face and get out and face the world.
☐ You can be just like Olivia, she was back to herself in no time.
☐ Think of how much more time you'll have to _____

THINGS WE *CAN* SAY

THIS IS COMFORT:

- [ ] Give a hug... actions are sometimes better than any words
- [ ] It is so good to see you / I'm so happy to see you
- [ ] I love you. I will be here every step of the way.
- [ ] Is there anything you want to talk about today?
- [ ] I saw ____ today and thought of you. Know that I'm here.
- [ ] I wish I knew what to say
- [ ] We'll get through this together.
- [ ] You are not alone. I am here for you and won't leave you.
- [ ] I'm so so sorry
- [ ] Take all the time you need
- [ ] I remember the time we___
- [ ] Do you remember when we____?
- [ ] You've had to deal with so much
- [ ] Do you feel like talking about it?
- [ ] It must be really hard.
- [ ] It hurts to know you are going through this.
- [ ] How has this week been so far?
- [ ] I can see the pain in your eyes
- [ ] That's terrible
- [ ] How awful
- [ ] No.....
- [ ] I was hoping it would be different
- [ ] You look like you can use a hug
- [ ] Share memories / any memories
- [ ] This must be so hard
- [ ] I'm thinking of you
- [ ] You are on my heart every single day
- [ ] Please know how much I care
- [ ] Tell me what these past few days have been like
- [ ] I will keep checking in on you (and mean it and do it)
- [ ] How can I pray for you?
- [ ] I have absolutely no idea how you're feeling right now, but I am here and I care

- [ ] I'm so glad you're my friend and I hurt when you hurt. Can we get together?
- [ ] I'll always be here for you
- [ ] I remember when....
- [ ] It's ok to be angry
- [ ] It sounds like it's not a very good day... do you want to tell me about it?
- [ ] Has anything good happened today?
- [ ] I haven't heard from you in awhile, is everything ok?
- [ ] If and when you want to talk, I'm here.
- [ ] I've noticed you don't seem yourself lately. Are you ok?
- [ ] I'm just checking in on you. How is today?
- [ ] I just want you to know that I have you on my heart, it seems like you're going through a rough time. I'm here for you.
- [ ] I know you're dealing with some stuff these days and please know that I'm here and I care.
- [ ] You've been missed at practice, is everything ok?
- [ ] Where have you been? I miss you. Are you ok?
- [ ] I know you're going through a lot. What do you need from me today?
- [ ] I'm worried about you. I'm here. How can I help?
- [ ] I'm not sure how to say this, but I sense something isn't right with you. Is there anything you want to talk about?
- [ ] What's up? I haven't heard from you in so long.
- [ ] I hope you know how special you are to me. Can we get together soon?
- [ ] You have the best smile and I haven't seen it in so long. What's going on?
- [ ] Whatever you are going through right now, always know you are not alone. Can we talk?
- [ ] I'm so glad you're my friend and I hurt when you hurt. Can we get together?

It is never too late to send condolences. Often a letter coming much later comes at the perfect time.
~Zig Ziglar

HANDS

When someone is struggling, truth is it may take some time for them to be ready to talk. This is when written words come to the rescue. You have more time to carefully craft exactly what you want to say and your words actually last longer. Good and kind written messages can be read and re-read over and over, to sustain someone who is broken and help make them feel whole again.

Messages of comfort and support over a sustained period of time also help lay a deep foundation of trust and friendship. Many little check ins and words of hope and encouragement can make a big difference in the life of someone feeling isolated and alone.

Please don't underestimate the power of the pen, or the computer keyboard or your thumbs up message on a screen. Written words matter. A lot.

PROS AND CONS OF DIFFERENT WRITTEN COMFORT

With so many different ways to send a personal caring written message of comfort, you really shouldn't have any excuse not to send one. And then another one. And another and another. You get the point.

MESSAGE	PROS	CONS	TIMING
GREETING CARD	Wonderful way to express your thoughts and to add your own personal message.	Not many - although a personal message is really where you can comfort.	Immediately upon hearing the news or when you suspect something is wrong. Often sending additional cards weeks and months later has the benefit of long term comfort.
WRITTEN LETTER	Personal form of comfort that is long lasting and always comes from and to the heart.	Takes concentrated effort.	ANYTIME
EMAIL	They offer an immediate contact and allow you to share your thoughts as long or short as you like.	May not be received as very personal. Also emails get buried and sometimes missed and forgotten.	Best for an immediate connection
TEXT	Wonderful way to provide a frequent check in. A super easy and effective way to stay in touch with someone long term.	People are typically busy and won't read and remember a long text	Texting is an excellent strategy to begin when they start feeling forgotten and alone.
SOCIAL MEDIA	Personal pictures and memories can be shared and preserved if the timing is right.	Can be hurtful to the one suffering if not posted correctly. Additionally messages can miss the "one to one" need for comfort when those leaving comments worry about how others will read it.	Follow the lead of the one suffering. If they are not posting about it, don't. It's their story.

5 GUIDELINES TO REMEMBER WHEN YOU ARE WRITING A MESSAGE OF COMFORT:

1. Start with the heart

Just as in spoken word, think about how you are caring for this person. Heart to heart.

2. Keep it one to one.

When writing your message, write it only to the person you are writing it for even if others will be included in your message.

3. Focus

Keep the focus on the person you are comforting. Refrain from sharing stories about how you can relate because of a similar situation. Don't include how this is affecting you or any updates with news from you. Your sole focus is to warm the heart of the one who is hurting.

4. Think back

Before you start to write, take a few minutes to recall your favorite times with this person. Think about what you like most about them. Think about how you would be feeling if you were them. Then write from there.

5. Keep at it

Check in often. Mark you calendar to check in with them again in the near future. Do not abandon them after one written message. They need you.

PAIGE'S STORY

There is no better person to demonstrate how written words can bring comfort than my sweet friend Paige, who used her words and her art to help recover from tragedy.

Paige was a first grader at Sandy Hook and a student of her favorite teacher ever, Vickie Soto. But on that fateful day she lost her beloved teacher along with her classmates, while escaping with her life. She carries a burden that neither you nor I can fathom. Her beautiful spirit is finding its way forward with many ways of therapy, love and support.

She has an eye for art and a heart that is sensitive, kind and always looking to others. I have watched over the years how she uses these gifts in the most beautiful ways.

When Paige decides she wants to comfort someone, she will review a list of people in her head and settle on the one that hits her heart that day. And then she will pause, think and plan. She will sketch out designs and carefully decide what words she will use to write a message.

It is not a quick random exercise for her. It is slow and thoughtful and incredibly intentional. I have watched many times as she has started over or changed direction if the words or image doesn't fit with the message she wants to convey.

Now in 8th grade, Paige estimates that she's comforted over 200 people since that first plaque 4 years ago. She is aware that her art skills continue to be refined and her words are maturing, but her process has never shifted, just deepened. Her heart has grown bigger and more confident as she has received love and comfort back from those she has comforted.

Some would call this Post Traumatic Growth. I think Paige would just call this finding her heart.

TEXTING COMFORT

The power of a check in text: "I so appreciate your text. My mother is having confusion and frightening hallucinations in the early evenings, making supper for my dad (who is not longer alive) and then angry when he doesn't come home and worrying about her kids saying "where are my babies?". It's common in Alzheimer's, but an added cruelty is that she eventually recognizes she was confused so it's doubly frightening for her. I've researched some solutions (sunlamp, more early day exercise, lots of lights in the evening so no shadows) and it helped this weekend! Thank you for checking in, it helps my burden." – L.R.

Texting can truly be one of the best and easiest ways to keep in touch with someone struggling. It's personal. One to one and quick. If done right, you can open someone's heart to accept more comfort and they can immediately respond with how they are or what they might need. You can change things up depending on the day and the mood by adding humor or understanding when needed. Many little text check ins can lay a wonderful trusting relationship with someone who needs a friend. When we think of the comfort jar and each text being a marble, it's a wonderful way to keep adding to the jar.

FIVE REASONS WHY TEXTING IS A GREAT WAY TO COMFORT:

1. It's not awkward

If you are someone in need of comfort, there is something really special about a kind, warm, funny or comforting text from a friend. It pops up and requires nothing but can grow into a beautiful conversation.

2. There are options

Don't feel like writing something? Send a Bitmoji or beautiful image. Link to a favorite song or find the perfect GIF. You can create a weekly themed check in like "Memory Monday" or "Thinking of you Thursday".

3. They add up

When you take the time to repeatedly check in on someone you let them know that you haven't forgotten about them. So few people take the time to do this, but the ones that do really stand out. It builds up a sense of trust and deepens your friendship.

4. It's one-to-one

It's just you and your friend. And that means a lot.

5. You can progressively go deeper

You can ask questions or offer to help with a specific task and they can quickly answer. A quick text can be one of the best ways to figure out "what now?".

5 *PITFALLS* OF TEXTING COMFORT:

As wonderful as texting can be, we do need to be careful that what we send, how often we send it and when we send texts is what your friend or acquaintance needs and appreciates. Remember these 5 pitfalls so that you don't overwhelm the person you are trying to help.

1.Danger of "group comfort"

It's best not to comfort in a group text chain. The one needing comfort wants to hear from each person individually. You also run the risk of "piling on" with similar stories and advice.

2. Don't overdo it

It's important to make sure the person you are comforting wants to receive texts of comfort from you. Always ask if it's ok to keep checking in.

3. Watch the mood

Don't try to cheer someone up if they are down.

4. Watch the time

Be sure to know the best time when to send your texts. It's important not to wake people with notifications when they are resting.

5. Keep the focus on them, not you

Keep the focus of the texts away from your own life until they open the door of wanting to hear what's going on with you. It will progress there, just wait for that door to open.

POSTING OF LOSS & TRAGEDY ON SOCIAL MEDIA

While I was in the final stages of finishing this book, I suffered a terrible loss. My sister Julie's wonderful husband Tom passed away. I grew up with Tom. Julie met him while I was in college and so I can barely remember a time when Tom wasn't in my life.

My parents were with me in Virginia when we got the news and we quickly rearranged our plans and set out to drive the 5 hours up to New York. Throughout the drive I was receiving texts from friends asking how Tom was. (I had a large community of friends who were praying for him in his last weeks and so would check in frequently).

On one of our stops along the way to New York, I decided to post on Facebook so those asking me how he was would hear the news. That way and I wouldn't have to let all my texts go unanswered. So I carefully crafted a post sharing what a wonderful man Tom was and what he meant to me and really all the right things to say to share memories of someone you love.

There was only one problem. And it's a big one. It wasn't my story to tell.

We were back on the road not even 10 minutes when I received a call from my sister asking if I could please take the post down. Pause and think about this situation. She had just lost her husband, hadn't fully wrapped her head around it, hadn't even given much thought as to how she was going to share the news and was now getting texts from people hearing the news from me.

I felt about as horrible as I could. Here I am writing a book on comfort and I'm the one that makes this very bad comfort mistake. I knew not to do this and yet I did it. For one reason - I didn't pause. I was focused on my own loss and how I wanted to remember my brother in law. But I failed to think of Julie first and the fact that this was not my story to tell. As a result I added to her pain.

I quickly took down my post before any more news spread. Julie then went about making sure Tom's network of friends heard from either her or another close friend. She reached out to a group of his closest friends asking them to help share the news to their networks. Instead of private phone calls, email and texts, one of the friends posted on Facebook and tagged Tom, which meant Tom's entire network of friends and family saw the post. Julie's heart broke when one of Tom's cousins commented on the post before the family was able to spread the news.

It made me realize just how easily this can happen and how much extra heartache is added to someone already grieving. In this case, my sister waited until an obituary was written and used that to share her news on social media. She used the time before that to reach those closest to Tom who deserved to hear from her or another family member or close friend. The best course of action to follow would have been to wait to see her first post and then share the news.

So please - do not be the one to rush to social media to share news that you know or hear. Allow time for the one closest to their life changing event to process their feelings and notify the important people in their life in the right way at the right time. Follow their lead.

5 GUIDELINES TO REMEMBER WHEN YOU ARE POSTING NEWS OF A LIFE CHANGING EVENT:

1. Start with the heart

Think about the event that just happened and who it is impacting. Many other hearts are involved.

2. Whose story is it to tell?

If this is not your story to tell, do not post anything. Fight the urge to be the sharer of news even if you are hurting from this event.

3. Follow the lead

Wait until the person closest to the event has shared the news publicly before you post of the event. Once the news has been shared by those most impacted, you can post.

4. When you do post

Keep the focus on positive, loving memories. Refrain from posting how this is personally impacting you if possible. Instead honor those who need to be honored and support those who need to be supported.

5. Go one to one

Follow up one to one with those most impacted. Check in often. Mark your calendar to check in with them again in the near future. Do not abandon them. They need you.

Connor's Story

My brother and I took our sons out of town for a camping weekend. On Saturday afternoon, my son and his cousins took my car to go out for ice cream. They didn't see the drunk driver run the red light as they crossed through the intersection. The car hit right where my son was driving. His cousins survived, but in a flash my son's precious life was gone.

The news was more than I could bear, but what followed made it worse. Not even 2 hours after the crash, one of my son's friends posted "RIP Josh" on his social media accounts, and this simple post stunned my whole family as the world heard about it before we had the chance to tell anyone. My own mother heard about her grandson dying through a text from a friend who was "so sorry to hear the news". There was simply no way to control the flow of the news once "RIP" was posted, and it haunts me to this day. I'm sure his friend was simply caught up in his own grief, but I don't think he understood what that post did to my family and I.

My son's story spread quickly through social media before any of us could catch our breath. His friends and teammates quickly sharing the news they heard from his friend caused our phones to blow-up with "thinking of you"s before we could begin to gather our own thoughts. Soon, media outlets and groups advocating for stricter drunk driving laws shared "their view" of what happened before anything was clear. His cousins, frozen in shock, couldn't cope with the combination of trauma and attention from social media and media outlets, and my wife and I no longer had control of Josh's memory.

All I kept thinking was "this is MY son, not yours, who are you to be telling this story without my permission?". I still can't come to terms with this. How does this happen?

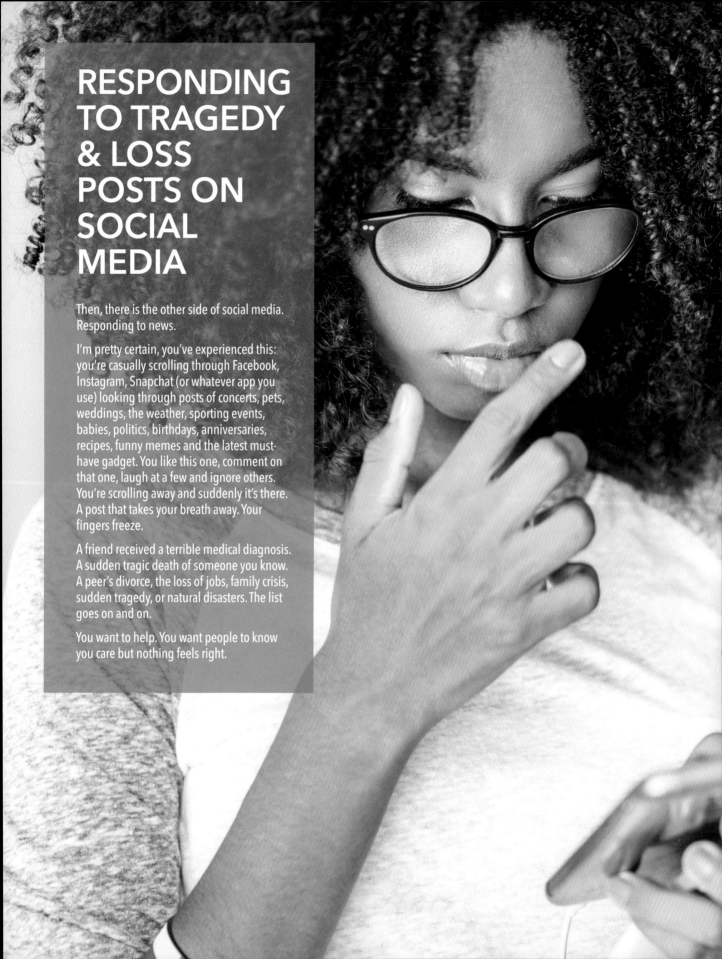

RESPONDING TO TRAGEDY & LOSS POSTS ON SOCIAL MEDIA

Then, there is the other side of social media. Responding to news.

I'm pretty certain, you've experienced this: you're casually scrolling through Facebook, Instagram, Snapchat (or whatever app you use) looking through posts of concerts, pets, weddings, the weather, sporting events, babies, politics, birthdays, anniversaries, recipes, funny memes and the latest must-have gadget. You like this one, comment on that one, laugh at a few and ignore others. You're scrolling away and suddenly it's there. A post that takes your breath away. Your fingers freeze.

A friend received a terrible medical diagnosis. A sudden tragic death of someone you know. A peer's divorce, the loss of jobs, family crisis, sudden tragedy, or natural disasters. The list goes on and on.

You want to help. You want people to know you care but nothing feels right.

10 TIPS FOR RESPONDING TO LIFE CHANGING EVENTS ON SOCIAL MEDIA

1. Pause

Take a breath and let this news sink in. This person is hurting and they need you. If someone is posting about their pain, it's like a door has been opened. They would not post if they would not want to hear from you.

2. Stay

Fight the urge to keep scrolling because you don't know what to say or do.

3. Start with your heart

Stop to really see the person that created the post. Think about what they need to hear. By reading the post as if it happened to you, you can identify more easily with what they are going through. And that will help you to know what to say and do. Avoid platitudes such as "RIP" and "Everything will be ok".

4. Like, heart, sad face or comment?

A well thought out and appropriate comment has the most value to someone and is the best choice. In this case, the poster will not be looking for how many likes they get or even how many sad face emojis they get. They are in need of words and love.

5. Keep it about them, not you

Don't tell them that you know how they feel (you don't) or compare their situation with something you experienced. This is a time to solely focus on them and what they need to hear to lift their heart.

6. Share a memory

It's always ok to share a memory in picture or words. Those are comments of the best kind.

7. Don't be a news spreader

This is not your story to tell. Support the person but don't spread the news unless you are asked to do so.

8. Go private

Send a private message, text, letter or a snail mail card. Pick up the phone and call, even if it's only to leave a message. When you reach out one to one instead of commenting publicly, it means more. It just does. It's only you and them and it changes how your message is received.

9. Do more

Everything for them has changed, their daily routine has been blown out the window. What more can you do for them? Do they need help? Do they need financial support or help with the kids? Can you help run errands for them or meet them for a cup of coffee? It's easy to assume that someone else will step up and take care of what they need. But it doesn't always work that way. People are all too busy now. If it's on your heart, then you are meant to help. Please do.

10. Remember them

People don't just "get over" the worst times in their lives. So, remember them and stay in touch. Don't ignore this when you see them. Write down the important dates and remind yourself to follow up again and again and again. It will mean a whole lot to them.

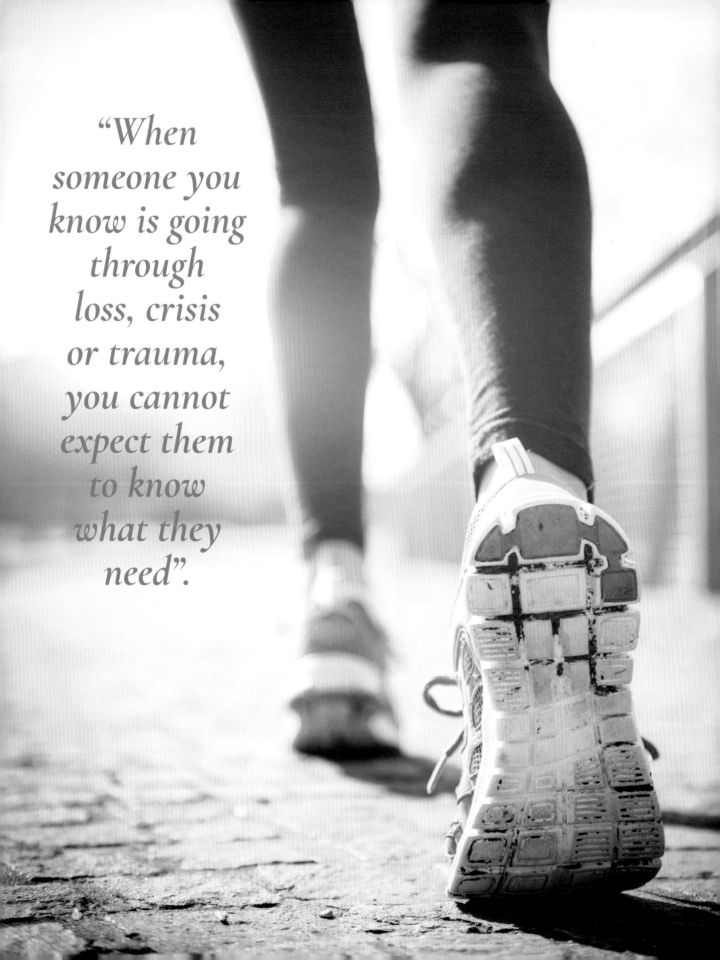

"When someone you know is going through loss, crisis or trauma, you cannot expect them to know what they need".

FEET

In April of 2013 I ran the Boston Marathon. Let me just say at the onset that I did not qualify to run this race. I didn't even start running until my late 40's and this was a huge stretch goal for me. I ran it as a charity runner, raising funds for a wonderful organization called buildOn, whose mission is to break the cycle of poverty, illiteracy and low expectations through service and education.

The training for this race was a good diversion for me. It was something to focus on and look forward to as I was immersed in the human destruction left behind after a mass shooting. I dedicated mile 26 to my new friends at Sandy Hook Elementary and I couldn't wait to share the adventure with them when it was over. Little did I know that I would be stopped just short of that 26th mile after two bombs went off. That I would wander 4 more miles through the streets of Boston lost, cold and confused, searching for my family. That I would be left to try to make sense of yet another tragedy.

The thing about being an ancillary survivor of a mass trauma is you think you're fine because you aren't physically injured. You survived. But you may not be ok. And you may not even realize it.

In the middle of the chaos, there was that one friend of mine who knew just what to do when I didn't know myself. Her name is Dot. "I'll meet you at your house and stay for a day or two" she texted me. "Dot, that's really sweet but you don't need to miss work for me, I'm fine really", I answered. But she wouldn't take no for an answer and when I arrived home Dot was there. She went grocery shopping and made some meals when I didn't even realize those were things I needed to do. She took my daughters wherever they needed to go. I was moving a little slow, not only because my legs were sore, but because my mind was not clear. I was unable to process things logically in my brain. Dot helped me think straight and her friendship and presence were the best gifts anyone could have given me at that time.

It was through all of this that I realized that all we **can** do is to try our best to do good. To go deeper and try harder. To focus our minds on all the good things around us instead of all of the darkness and tragedy. And to intentionally act and be there to help. Even if it's awkward.

Dot didn't forget about me after she went back home. She texted me frequently to see how I was. She called me now and then and we got together more often than we had before this happened. She became an even closer friend to me.

The abrupt ending of the Boston Marathon actually opened a new door. The door of realization that helping others one on one is the key. Showing up again and again and again.

We can all be more like Dot.

HALF OF LIFE IS SHOWING UP

When I returned home from cancer surgery, I was showered with love and attention from family and friends. It was wonderful, a bit overwhelming and then it was over. Within a week, the flood of attention became a trickle. If not for a few friends who stopped by for coffee or to play chess, it was as if I'd been forgotten. I now make a point of checking in on recovering or homebound people after the crowds have gone back to their daily lives. – Ed D.

When someone is going through a major change, crisis or trauma, it is almost too much to just get up and through the day. All of the daily needs of life are nearly impossible to keep up with.

The good news? This is where friendships are made and deepened. It's when people feel forgotten and burdened, that the smallest gesture will mean the most. Use this next section to find things that you can do. Circle or check the items that resonate with you. And then do them. Again and again and again.

COMFORT ACTION TIPS

Before you set out to deliver that meal or offer to mow their lawn or pretty much take on any of the tasks listed, read through these 8 tips. Our intentions are almost always really good, so let's make sure that they are executed well.

8 TIPS FOR COMFORT ACTIONS

☐ **Lead with your heart**–Sometimes when we sign up to do something for someone we realize we are short on time and it turns into a stressful action. Try not to let that happen by always remembering how much this will mean.

☐ **Greeting**–Decide first if they want to be seen. Many times they do not wish to be disturbed. However if they have agreed to see you, please greet them with a smile and a simple greeting like "It's wonderful to see you."

☐ **Permission**–Always seek permission to do anything in their home, running errands or financial assistance. Everyone views things very different and it's important to respect that.

☐ **Keep Going**–Help can take the form of small gestures or large tasks and is needed so much longer than most people realize.

☐ **No Expectations**–Don't expect thanks or recognition for what you are doing and sometimes it's good to tell them that.

☐ **Be sensitive to their needs**–Don't be overeager and overstep what they need.

☐ **Timing**–Be aware of their current mindset and connect and comfort accordingly. Too much too soon is more harmful than helpful. Be mindful that well after the initial outpouring of support, there is a void and that will be a wonderful time to offer help as well.

☐ **Follow Up**– Always follow up to see what more you can do.

FOOD SUPPORT

"Thank you so much, this is really good. Last night I had jelly beans for dinner." ~ true story.

When someone is going through a challenging time, struggle, crisis or change, there is simply nothing better than getting good food. Most likely this will not be a priority for them and we all know that we feel worse when we don't eat well. So help them eat well.

FIVE THINGS TO KNOW ABOUT MEAL NEEDS

1. Don't ever assume that they don't need meals if they are not on an organized meal trains. One of the best ways you can touch base with someone is to text a simple "Hey I made a huge pot of chicken noodle soup, can I bring some over?"
2. Meal needs go on for a very long time.
3. The refrigerator and kitchen cupboards will get full of leftovers and old foods. The help of a friend to keep the fridge clean is a big blessing to those hurting.
4. Get creative and think of non-dinner needs. Dropping off breakfast or a mid afternoon snack is a welcome surprise.
5. Don't forget the people at work. They may be short on funds and short on time. Why not offer to bring an extra lunch for someone in the office. Or better yet, just surprise them or anonymously drop off something you know they'd like.

USEFUL TIPS:

- ☐ Don't plan to talk with the family when you drop off the meal.
- ☐ Be on time. The family is planning their schedule around this meal.
- ☐ Follow dietary restrictions - many people can be on special diets. Honor that. Don't send salty foods to someone on a low salt diet. Don't send meats to a vegan. Check for allergies.
- ☐ Ask about foods that get sent a lot. Lasagna and pastas tends to be favorites that can get old fast.
- ☐ Healthy fresh meals are always extremely appreciated but they require more preparation. Fresh fruits and vegetables. Lean meats. Make the time if you can.
- ☐ Include something light and fresh like a salad as part of the meal, and some sort of treat—like a pint of ice cream. If there are children, consider some fun foods just for them.
- ☐ Don't drop off anything that needs to be assembled and prepared.
- ☐ Consider making a meal in their home if they would like the company.

"We went out to retrieve our meal train dinner in the cooler on our porch. When we opened the lid we found 2 boxes of pasta, 2 jars of Ragu, a head of lettuce and a bottle of salad dressing. This was not helpful."

TOP THINGS TO CONSIDER WHEN PARTICIPATING IN A MEAL TRAIN

If you can organize one, thank you. If you only participate in one, thank you. Both matter. There are some things to remember though, according to the popular site Meal Train, here are some guidelines:

☐ If there are open calendar days after your delivery, make enough for leftovers. Freezable meals are also nice.

☐ Don't forget the extras like drinks, condiments, and salad dressing.

☐ If you are having something delivered (e.g. pizza), make sure to pay and tip in advance.

☐ If possible, deliver your meal in a recyclable or reusable container.

☐ Be sure to label any items that you would like returned. Include a large paper bag with your name on it that the recipient can use to store your items until you can coordinate a pick-up date.

☐ Include clear preparation instructions, i.e. "Bake for 1 hour at 350 degrees."

☐ Consider sharing a link to your recipe in the "Notes" section of your meal booking so the recipient can know the ingredients.

☐ As a nice added bonus, bring breakfast food for the following morning, such as muffins, bagels, and fruit salad.

☐ If possible, text the recipient that you are on your way. A little heads up can go a long way.

☐ If you don't live nearby or can't cook, consider sending a Grubhub or Uber Eats gift card.

TAKING CARE OF THEM

Caring for another is one of the most loving things we can do. Here are some ideas that you can adapt in your own situation. Sometimes they will want to be left alone and so here are things you can do when that's the case:

- ☐ Give a personal care package filled with all of their favorite things whenever you can
- ☐ Take note of all of what they love to eat and drink and do and make sure they get them.
- ☐ Be there with daily encouragement even if it's only a simple text
- ☐ Don't ever let them think you forgot about them – check in frequently
- ☐ Send love whenever you can
- ☐ Give them your favorite book of hope – highlight sections you want to share – write in the margins
- ☐ Invite them out to events and meals – frequently - even if they don't want to go. They will appreciate being asked.
- ☐ Gather friends to write "pick me up" notes and send them each week.
- ☐ Be prepared for months / years of support
- ☐ Don't ever assume they are "over it" and have "moved on" from a live changing event.
- ☐ Write out the prayers you are praying for them and send them
- ☐ Create a quiet "time out" space in their house - ask if o.k. to pull the shades, fill with lavender or candles, flowers. Have a beautiful journal or meditation books available.
- ☐ Look through the rest of this sections to find specific things to do to help.

DOING THINGS WITH THEM

Sometimes people would love companionship but prefer not to feel pressure to talk about their struggles. Doing activities together is a wonderful way to show friendship and help them get their minds off of things for a bit.

- ☐ Cook a meal with them
- ☐ Play a game / Do a puzzle
- ☐ Take for a Mani / Pedi
- ☐ Go to a movie
- ☐ Go for wine or coffee
- ☐ Go for walk or run or hike
- ☐ Buy them lunch
- ☐ Go for a nice long drive
- ☐ Take them grocery shopping and make it fun... buy some silly things for them
- ☐ Go for haircuts together
- ☐ Gather friends for a night together
- ☐ Take them to worship
- ☐ Bring over movies and popcorn – whatever the mood calls for and laugh and cry with them
- ☐ Take them for ice cream
- ☐ Go sing karaoke
- ☐ Work out at the gym with them
- ☐ Learn a craft together liked stained glass or knitting
- ☐ Sign up to take a class with them Park and Recreation, Bible Study, Workshop, Library

"How we walk with the broken speaks louder than how we sit with the great."

HOSPITAL STAYS

When someone is experiencing an extended hospital stay, think of comfort for them as well as their hospital room (and don't forget their home needs too)

- ☐ Bring good healthy food they can eat and they like
- ☐ Read a book with them
- ☐ Bring them flowers, it never gets old
- ☐ Give mani / pedi's
- ☐ Have a pre-surgery party
- ☐ Bring new PJ's & slippers
- ☐ Be a consistent in person prayer partner
- ☐ Bring decorations for the drabby hospital room
- ☐ Bring a new comfy blanket
- ☐ Bring a "party in a box" and have a little celebration
- ☐ Lotion their feet and hands
- ☐ Bring an iPad or large screen device and set them up with Netflix / Hulu / Favorite Shows
- ☐ Program their favorite music and podcasts on their phone or other device.
- ☐ Arrange a therapy/comfort dog visit
- ☐ Bring a movie to watch with them. Bring popcorn.
- ☐ Bring photo albums and other memories from home
- ☐ Spend a few extra minutes thanking the nurses and aids
- ☐ Ask if they need help with any insurance paperwork

SIDE NOTE: Please consider everyone in the hospital when you visit. Many patients have no visitors and medical staff can feel overworked and unappreciated. There is plenty of comfort that needs to go around in our hospitals.

HOUSEHOLD SUPPORT

The daily needs don't stop when tough things happen, that's where help is truly needed:

- ☐ Clean the House:
    - Change the sheets
    - Wash the sheets/towels
    - Vacuum
    - Clean the bathrooms
    - Pick Up Toys
    - Clean out the fridge
    - Load / unload dishwasher
    - Clean up dead flowers
- ☐ Do the laundry
- ☐ Be the handyman - there are always things around the house that need fixing.
- ☐ Water and care for of all of the house plants
- ☐ Make meals in the home for them
- ☐ Fill the house with good smells
- ☐ Help organize and bring calm
- ☐ Help Keep Traditions Alive
    - Holidays
    - Birthdays
    - Valentines Day
    - Celebrations
- ☐ Plug in Air Fresheners / Light candles

"After my husband had a stroke, it's impossible to keep up with my house. Things keep breaking and I don't have the money or time to take care of them. It just adds to my burden and stress"

DAILY ERRANDS & NEEDS

Going out and getting the basic things done is challenging for those struggling and adds stress. You can help:

- ☐ Dry Cleaning Pick Up / Drop
- ☐ Fruit, Veggies & Dairy weekly
- ☐ Groceries
- ☐ Drive to doctor appts
- ☐ Write thank you notes for them
- ☐ Any shopping needs
- ☐ Start the car for them when it's below freezing
- ☐ Yard work /weeding/raking
- ☐ Fill their gas tank
- ☐ Bring in their mail everyday
- ☐ Help sort out junk mail
- ☐ Wash their car
- ☐ Bring in fresh flowers
- ☐ Empty Wastebaskets
- ☐ Help them keep kids doctors appointments
- ☐ Get dog groomed
- ☐ Walk the dog for them
- ☐ Pick up doogie doo in yard
- ☐ Take Garbage in and out each week
- ☐ Snow plowing / shoveling

"My friend Chelsea brings me fresh produce every Sunday evening. It brings me so much joy and helps me eat healthy for the week."

FINANCIAL SUPPORT

Unexpected situations can be costly and most likely aren't planned for, this can create so many added stressors for those in crisis:

- ☐ Start a Go Fund Me page for them
- ☐ Contribute to or fully pay bills for them: Utilities/ Phone Bill/ Rent
- ☐ Help to organize insurance or any other paperwork
- ☐ Help make calls to sort out bills if needed
- ☐ Give flights and hotel rooms as needed
- ☐ Gas Cards
- ☐ Gift Cards to where they shop for groceries etc...
- ☐ Start a Vacation fund and help get people donating
- ☐ Create a fundraiser
- ☐ Pay for House Cleaner

"A colleague gave me miles to buy a plane ticket home that I desperately needed but couldn't afford"

KID STUFF

- [ ] Make a card or special gift for their parent(s)
- [ ] Take them for ice cream
- [ ] Visit the library
- [ ] Host a birthday party
- [ ] Plan play dates
- [ ] Take them to the movies
- [ ] Take them to a concert or sporting event
- [ ] Offer to babysit
- [ ] Drive them to/from school
- [ ] Take over carpool duties for sports/ hobbies
- [ ] Help with homework or tutor them
- [ ] Blow bubbles
- [ ] Take them shopping for shoes, clothes or school supplies
- [ ] Bring ingredients and cook dinner with the kids
- [ ] Take them to church
- [ ] Have them over to your house and do something special and fun.
- [ ] Send YOUR kids over to bake cookies or play a favorite game.
- [ ] Have a karaoke night
- [ ] Build a fire pit and make s'mores
- [ ] Plant or tend a garden
- [ ] Create a dream board with them

"My friend came over and helped my son with his homework when I was sick. It made all the difference."

-LEIGH, 39

GRIEF SUPPORT *FOR* THEM

"When my friends gave me a scrapbook full of pictures and stories of my dad , I was so overcome with emotion I didn't know what to say. It was the nicest thing anyone could have done for me."

- ☐ Collect and preserve memories
  - Memorial Facebook Page
  - Email friends and family for memories and pictures and make an album
  - Create something for the memorial
  - Share a memory a week
  - Help to create photo albums and frame their favorite pictures of the deceased
  - Have a quilt made from some favorite clothes of the deceased
- ☐ Create a journal "Love Letters to_____" to help them capture memories and moments when they come to mind... writing letters to their loved one to help ease the pain.
- ☐ Bake the favorite foods of the person who died... fill the house with those smells and play their favorite music. Eat with them and share memories if they want. Bring Kleenex.
- ☐ Make a note of the anniversaries of events and be available specifically on those days.
- ☐ Keep friends and family aware of the ongoing need to keep the memories alive and celebrate the life lost.
- ☐ Don't change anything about the way you interact with them. If they are on a text chain or email with them, keep sending them emails until they ask you to stop.
- ☐ Keep asking them what support they need around the house, with their kids, with their errands.

GRIEF SUPPORT *WITH* THEM

When someone is grieving, patience and love are the key things they will need from you:

- ☐ Just be there. And listen. And love them. Say the name.
- ☐ Hug them. As often as they will let you.
- ☐ Show up often and help them with the activities they have to do
- ☐ Go for a walk whenever possible and ask to share favorite memories
- ☐ Help sort out cards / funeral planning / guest lists / out of town travelers
- ☐ Help them with the belongings of the deceased whenever they are ready. Don't rush this.
- ☐ Invite them to things you are going to. At first they may say no, but keep asking. People love to be invited.
- ☐ Sort out the most important memories with them and preserve them.
- ☐ Arrange to share some of the items with those closest to the deceased and help them package up and deliver.
- ☐ Offer to find homes for the rest of the items and share stories of where everything went and how it's being used.

"I really do want to go places and do things. Some days I feel like I can do this and other days I am buried under a wave of sadness. Please don't give up on me."

SOUL

We have so far addressed comfort for the mind and body. It would be impossible to write a book on comfort and leave out the soul. The faith element. For people of faith, they rely on spiritual support whether it be of prayer or prayer services, meditation, pilgrimages, worship or bible study to get them through. However, if you are not a person of faith, you can skip this chapter and move directly to the final section of the book where you will create your own comfort plan.

I guess you could say that there was a reason I was ready to help in the halls of Sandy Hook Elementary in 2013. My journey of comfort can actually be traced back 9 years earlier, when another tragedy called me to comfort.

It was in the spring of 2004. I walked into church one sunny crisp day and felt the feeling I would later experience all too frequently. The feeling of the oxygen being sucked out of the building, the stillness, the darkness, the sadness and shock.

Beautiful 16 month old Alec Nelson had been tragically killed by a freak accident. Sweet little Alec, the same age as my daughter Audrey. There were no words. Just intense pain and unbelief.

At the time, I didn't know the Nelsons all too well, but I was asked to play piano at the funeral. That simple act gave me the privilege of witnessing an extraordinary outpouring of love and faith and support for this beautiful family. I sat there on a piano bench watching in awe as Bill Nelson, Alec's father, stood in front of a packed church with grace and peace. Talking about Alec, and his faith, and his trust that God would work things together for good. He used this most darkest of times to share hope. How does one do that?

I remember like yesterday leaving that funeral and driving home. The green leaves were just starting to pop out, the sun beamed through my sunroof onto my hands on the steering wheel and my mind completely fixated on how I could help this family. These beautiful people I hardly knew. I believe with my whole heart that God put it on my heart to help.

"He used the darkest of times as an opportunity to share hope. How does one do that?"

It wasn't only a nice thing to do, it was my job. I was given an assignment. When something is put so strong on your heart, how can you ignore it.

I am a Christian and I believe this is all a part of our purpose in life. It's what brings us joy and it's what brings us our own comfort and strength. We have never been promised a perfect world. In fact we are told that in this world we would have trouble. But we also know that this world is not the end of our story. We are basically walking with each other thru life to our final home. Picking each other up. Taking each others hands and holding each other up when we don't have the strength to stand ourselves.

When I look back on this situation and what faith did here, I first see that faith gave Bill the peace and strength to stand up and give hope. I then see that faith put the desire on my heart to help and gave me the motivation and words to show up again and again. I watched as Bill & his beautiful wife Adriann relied on their faith to find the strength to go forward each and every day.

Comforting the Nelson family brought me comfort and grew my faith. This helping gave comfort to the Nelson family and grew their faith. And now, 15 years and many many moments of caring and prayer later, I have a beautiful faith filled friendship with a family I hadn't known before this happened.

That is the Soul Circle of Comfort.

The Five Steps to Soul Comfort

These are adapted to my Christian beliefs and practices, please feel free to adapt to your own practices:

1. Be Aware – Pray for God to grow your desire to help and to open your eyes to those needing comfort.

2. Respond to the call – When someone is put on your heart to help, know that God has prepared you in advance to do this job. You are ready and capable. No one else can do the role that is put on your heart.

3. Walk with them – Recognize that you are in this for the long haul. Comfort is not a one and done task. This person or persons needs you and your time for months and years to come.

4. Pray for them – Keep them covered in prayer. Pray for them and with them. Add them to prayer chains if they agree.

5. Give gratitude to God for for being entrusted with this assignment and for growing your friendship and faith through this process.

"We are what we repeatedly do. Excellence then is not an act, but a habit."

– *Aristotle*

PART FOUR

Creating Your Personal Comfort Response Plan

MY PERSONAL PLAN: APPLYING THE SKILL

Helping others in need is not
only at the soul of our humanity;
It is what gives meaning to life

In the first section of Paws To Comfort you learned what dogs do that makes them such good comforters and why humans should be more like them. Section two gave you a better understanding of why giving comfort can be awkward and how changes our society has experienced in the area of human care make giving comfort even more difficult. Finally, in section three you learned that everyone needs comfort, why we need to change our mindset around comfort and what makes a good comforter.

Equipped with all this knowledge – you are now ready to make comfort work for you. Section four will guide you through creating your own comfort plan so that you can start to put comfort marbles into the jars of others – one marble at a time.

Just as everyone wants to be comforted differently, you have your own unique set of strengths that you can use to help those needing your love and support. A key goal is to help you identify areas that you can work on to make giving comfort even less awkward going forward. Once you have assessed yourself and start intentionally giving comfort it will eventually become your new normal.

We believe comforting should be comfortable and that means it fits you and your style – so let's get started!

This section is broken out into 3 areas to create your very own comfort plan.

1. You will assess your comfort style strengths and weaknesses, likes and dislikes.

2. You will recap these assessments and develop your "Awkward Zone" and "Comfort Zone" summaries.

3. Using your summaries you can create comfort goals that will help you push through your Awkward Zone while strengthening your Comfort Zone. To measure progress you will create and track an action plan to ensure you are meeting these goals.

Let's get comforting!

ASSESS YOUR COMFORT SKILLS

WHAT DOGS TEACH US

We can begin to learn how to comfort by observing our dogs. Please grade how you yourself do with these things that dogs do well

	NOT SO GOOD									I'M GREAT AT THIS!
I recognize when others are hurting	1	2	3	4	5	6	7	8	9	10
I put others first	1	2	3	4	5	6	7	8	9	10
I am present when around others	1	2	3	4	5	6	7	8	9	10
I don't judge or hold grudges	1	2	3	4	5	6	7	8	9	10
I don't need words to comfort	1	2	3	4	5	6	7	8	9	10
I comfort others even if I don't know them	1	2	3	4	5	6	7	8	9	10
I am never too busy for others	1	2	3	4	5	6	7	8	9	10
I show up when I am needed	1	2	3	4	5	6	7	8	9	10
I bring joy	1	2	3	4	5	6	7	8	9	10
I always assume the best in others	1	2	3	4	5	6	7	8	9	10
I Paws and rest when needed	1	2	3	4	5	6	7	8	9	10
I take time to play	1	2	3	4	5	6	7	8	9	10
I do this every single day	1	2	3	4	5	6	7	8	9	10

THE CASE FOR COMFORT

When you open your eyes to the needs all around us and realize you can do something about it, your motivation to learn this skill will change.

What three *trends* stick out most to you? (refer to pages 54-60)

TREND   **WHY IT STICKS OUT**

What three *statistics* stick out most to you? (refer to pages 68-69)

STATISTIC   **WHY IT STICKS OUT**

Barriers To Comfort

*Check up to 5 of these reasons why you
don't initiate comforting in the first place.*

It's UNcomfortABLE – It
doesn't come naturally
to me so I avoid it

Desire to Fix It – I want to
give advice and then the
conversation is short

Fear – "I'm afraid I'll ____",
so I didn't say anything

It's Work – I'm so busy and
I just don't have the time

I'm not good at it- Someone
else can and will do it better.

It's too overwhelming
– I have so many of my
own problems, I can't
take on more

Lack of Awareness –
I assuming people are
ok and have moved on

Regret – It's been so long,
and I didn't do anything. I
feel terrible. It's too late.

Caregiving Fatigue – I've
done all I can, I've reached
the end of my helping rope.

Feeling Unappreciated –
I don't think they've even
noticed anything I've done.

Moving on – My relationship
with this person is different,
I will find new friends.

Lack of Knowledge – I want
to help but have no clue
what to do.

You Know Him Better –
I sometimes ask friends how
someone is doing instead of
doing something myself

Circle the 3 (or more) words that most
apply to you when you think of comfort.
Using these words, create your own
description of what comfort is to you:

_____
_____
_____
_____
_____
_____
_____
_____
_____

The Supermarket Scenario

You run into someone in the supermarket who you know is going through a hard time: Circle 5 responses that most apply to you

I don't know what to say, so I rush through the encounter or avoid them all together by going to the next aisle	I want to help and talk to them but then in my nervousness I talk too much and can say things that are probably not helpful.	I will share difficult things going on in my own life so that they know they aren't the only one going through a tough time. Misery loves company.	I feel guilty for not having done more. I get uncomfortable thinking I've let them down and assume it's too late to do anything.	I will assume that they want space and so I will intentionally go to the next aisle.
I want to cheer them up	I want to help them by telling them what helped me when I went through something similar.	I will talk about random things, avoiding the subject, because I don't want to upset them.	I can have thoughts like: "They are making too much out of this. They need to think happy thoughts."	I will neglect to follow up with them after leaving the store.
I tell them "let me know how I can help" without having anything specific in mind.	If they have suffered a loss, I don't feel comfortable bringing up the name of the person who passed away.	I might think that enough time has passed and it's time they put this behind them and focus on the rest of their lives.	I have been known to be there for someone in the beginning of their crisis or loss but over time don't focus much on their circumstances.	I think in my head "Well at least people can see that you're going through a hard time. If you only knew what I was going through."

....

MY COMFORT STRENGTHS

	NOT SO GOOD									I'M GREAT AT THIS!
Listener	1	2	3	4	5	6	7	8	9	10
Conversationalist	1	2	3	4	5	6	7	8	9	10
Seeing those who are in pain	1	2	3	4	5	6	7	8	9	10
Meeting new people	1	2	3	4	5	6	7	8	9	10
Staying in touch with people I care about	1	2	3	4	5	6	7	8	9	10
Have extra time on my hands	1	2	3	4	5	6	7	8	9	10
Having purpose in my life	1	2	3	4	5	6	7	8	9	10
Having patience	1	2	3	4	5	6	7	8	9	10
Bringing people together	1	2	3	4	5	6	7	8	9	10
I am a calm & peaceful person with not much stress	1	2	3	4	5	6	7	8	9	10
I know my limits & don't take on too much	1	2	3	4	5	6	7	8	9	10

Where Do I Want To Focus Giving Comfort?

The number of people needing support can be overwhelming–it's important to focus your effort on areas where you feel most comfortable. Circle the areas where you feel most equipped and/or motivated to help:

LOSS
Loved one
Spouse
Parent
Child
Miscarriage/Stillbirth
Pet

PHYSICAL HEALTH
Hospitalization
Terminal Illness
Upcoming tests / awaiting
diagnosis
Chronic Pain / Injury / Illness
Severe Injury/loss of
mobilization
Homebound/Institutionalized
Special needs – person/
parents/loved ones
Loss of function – hearing,
seeing, ambulatory
Bed Ridden Pregnancies

MENTAL HEALTH
Anxiety
Depression
Self-Harm
Obsessive Compulsive
Disorder
Anger Management
Addictions
Mood disorders
Eating Disorders

EXTREME CONCERNS
Legal action
False Rumors
Homelessness

RELATIONSHIP CRISIS
Severe conflict with others
Divorce/infidelity/breakup
Rebellious Teen and Adult
children
Parenting Crisis
Family member in prison
Unwanted Pregnancy
Infertility
Families separated due to work

LOSS OF PURPOSE/ WORK/DREAMS
Loss of job
Loss of financial security
Mid life Crisis
Failed business proposal/plan
Unemployed
Job in crisis (impending layoffs,
downsizing)
Bankruptcy

THOSE WHO ENDURE HARDSHIP SERVING OTHERS
Doctors
Nurses
Clergy
Hospice Staff
Social Workers
Mental health professionals
Teachers
First Responders/Crisis and
Disaster Response
Fire
Police
Veterans and Families

CRISIS / TRAUMA RESPONSE
Natural Disasters – Hurricane/
Tornado/Flood/Earthquake
House/Car/Business
destruction
Mass trauma / terrorist events
Crisis Recovery
PTSD

CAREGIVERS
Children with disabilites
Parents with memory loss or
illness
Terminally ill family member
Spouse with severe illness
Children with illness or
addictions

LIFESTYLE CHANGES
Religion
Gender
Sexuality
Living Location
Empty Nesters
Moving
Adoption
Foster

EXTREME HOPELESSNESS
Bullying
Extreme Stress
Discouragement/Loss of
Hope/Sadness/Rejection/
Unforgiveness
Hidden Hurts

The Comfort Filter Test

If you think through these 5 points before you being talking, you will never have to worry about saying the wrong thing. Refer to page 150. Fill in the blanks:

P

A

U

S

E

WHAT TO SAY / NOT TO SAY
Read through the examples of word usage on page 154-158.
Fill in the phrases below that resonate with you

My 5 personal phrases that I'm guilty of and need to avoid

1

2

3

4

5

My 5 personal phrases I can say that resonate with me

1

2

3

4

5

Full Body Of Comfort

EARS – LISTENING

In your normal daily life, how good are you at listening to those around you in pain?
Circle which applies to you:

No matter how busy I am, I can shut everything out and focus on listening to the person I am engaged with. I actually feel better when I help them and it gives me energy to keep going.	I try to always remember to talk to people I encounter but sometimes I'm just too busy	I mostly go through my day focusing on the needs of me and my family	I am so overworked and stressed right now that I can't even accomplish what I need to do for myself and my family.

EYES – SEEING

In your normal daily life, how good are you at seeing to those around you in pain?
Circle which applies to you:

I make it a point to be aware and look people in the eye and greet them	I try to always remember to talk to people I encounter but sometimes I'm just too busy	I mostly go through my day focusing on the needs of me and my family	I am so overworked and stressed right now that I can't even accomplish what I need to do for myself and my family.

MOUTH – SAYING

What percentage of communication has to do with the words you say? (Refer to page 144.)

%

HANDS – WRITING

How I rate myself sending written words of comfort

	NOT SO GOOD									I'M GREAT AT THIS!
Sending a card	1	2	3	4	5	6	7	8	9	10
Writing a letter	1	2	3	4	5	6	7	8	9	10
Sending an email	1	2	3	4	5	6	7	8	9	10
Responding to a tragic social media post of someone you know	1	2	3	4	5	6	7	8	9	10
Sending texts / Snapchats / Instant messages one to one	1	2	3	4	5	6	7	8	9	10

....

FEET – GIFTS OF ACTION

Giving comfort to others should be enjoyable! The best way to make it that way is by doing things you love to do with or for others. Take a look at this list and think about your own house and your own life. What do you like to do?

	NOT SO GOOD									I'M GREAT AT THIS!
Baking / Cooking	1	2	3	4	5	6	7	8	9	10
Gardening	1	2	3	4	5	6	7	8	9	10
Sewing / Quilting / Knitting	1	2	3	4	5	6	7	8	9	10
Painting / Drawing / Coloring	1	2	3	4	5	6	7	8	9	10
Photography	1	2	3	4	5	6	7	8	9	10
Music/ Musician	1	2	3	4	5	6	7	8	9	10
Shopping	1	2	3	4	5	6	7	8	9	10
Organizing Parties or Project	1	2	3	4	5	6	7	8	9	10
Playing Cards / Games	1	2	3	4	5	6	7	8	9	10
Fixing things around the house	1	2	3	4	5	6	7	8	9	10
Taking care of Pets	1	2	3	4	5	6	7	8	9	10
Spiritual Support / Prayer Partner	1	2	3	4	5	6	7	8	9	10
Keeping my house clean	1	2	3	4	5	6	7	8	9	10
Keeping up with laundry	1	2	3	4	5	6	7	8	9	10

WHO DO I WORK BEST WITH?

Rate yourself on what age group you are most comfortable helping:

	NOT SO GOOD									I'M GREAT AT THIS!
Working with young children	1	2	3	4	5	6	7	8	9	10
Working with Middle School / High School age youth	1	2	3	4	5	6	7	8	9	10
Working with young adults	1	2	3	4	5	6	7	8	9	10
Working with adults	1	2	3	4	5	6	7	8	9	10
Working with families	1	2	3	4	5	6	7	8	9	10
Working with the elderly	1	2	3	4	5	6	7	8	9	10

....

MY FAVORITE WAYS TO COMMUNICATE: RANK 1-10
Texting - Phone Calls - Sending Cards - Writing Letters - Emails - Social Media - Face To Face - Snapchat - Facetime On Phone – Skype On Computer - Group Activities

1

2

3

4

5

6

7

8

9

10

Finding Time To Comfort

IDENTIFYING MY DISTRACTIONS

Estimated Number of Hours I Spend Each Week (and consider for a moment that many of these didn't exist 15 years ago):

ACTIVITY	HOURS PER WEEK	IS THIS OK? (CIRCLE ONE)		HOURS I COULD USE TO COMFORT
FACEBOOK		YES	NO	
INSTAGRAM		YES	NO	
SNAPCHAT		YES	NO	
NETFLIX OR OTHER STREAMING		YES	NO	
PINTEREST		YES	NO	
MINDLESS WEB SURFING		YES	NO	
TV/ MOVIES		YES	NO	
READING BOOKS, MAGAZINES, NEWS		YES	NO	
UNNECESSARY BUSYNESS		YES	NO	
TOTAL				

MY WEEK: WHEN I CAN SET ASIDE TIME

Check the windows of time where you can prioritize reaching out to others:

	M	T	W	T	F	S	S
6-8AM	☐	☐	☐	☐	☐	☐	☐
8-10AM	☐	☐	☐	☐	☐	☐	☐
10-12PM	☐	☐	☐	☐	☐	☐	☐
12-2PM	☐	☐	☐	☐	☐	☐	☐
2-4PM	☐	☐	☐	☐	☐	☐	☐
4-6PM	☐	☐	☐	☐	☐	☐	☐
6-8PM	☐	☐	☐	☐	☐	☐	☐
8-10PM	☐	☐	☐	☐	☐	☐	☐

It's The Things You Leave Undone
by Adelaide Proctor

It isn't the thing you do dear,
It's the thing you leave undone,
That gives you the bitter heartache
At the setting of the sun:
The tender word unspoken,
The letter you did not write,
The flower you might have sent, dear,
Are your haunting ghosts at night.

The stone you might have lifted
Out of your brothers way,
The bit of heartfelt counsel
You were hurried too much to say;

The loving touch of the hand, dear,
The gentle and winsome tone,
That you had no time or thought for,
With troubles enough of your own.

These little acts of kindness,
So easily out of mind,
These chances to be angels,
Which even mortals find
They come in nights of silence,
To take away the grief,
When hope is faint and feeble,
And a drought has stopped belief

For life is all too short, dear.
And sorrow is all too great,
To allow our slow compassion
That tarries until too late.
And it's not the thing you do, dear,

It's the thing you leave undone,
That gives you the bitter heartache,
At the setting of the sun.

....

Adelaide Proctor committed herself to progressive, philanthropic work, arguing for women's equality in property rights, employment and education. She supported Catholic widows and orphans through the Providence Row Night Refuge and was active in the Society to Promote the Employment of Women. In the last ten years of her life, before her early death at thirty-nine, poetry, campaigning for the rights of women and social reform were her focus

Putting My Comfort Skills To Action

SETTING GOALS

Now that you've finished your assessments and found your awkward and your comfort, please take a moment to pause and study your results. This is you. The wonderful, fabulous unique you. Just as our program participants have never made the same plaque in over 25,000 creations, no one will have these same assessment results – they are yours! Cherish that and use this information to guide your way forward as you create your own monthly comfort plan to make an intentional difference in the lives of those around you who need you.

The following pages allow you to create your own unique monthly path of comfort. The monthly planning sheets will help you to organize and keep track of the people in your life that you are helping.

Follow these steps each month:

1. Pick three areas in both your Awkward Zone and your Comfort Zone that you wish to focus on this month. Maybe it's improving your listening skills. Or maybe it's using your skill of baking to take cookies to some people you know who would love to be cheered up and can use a friend. Write these goals on your monthly goal sheet and come up with specific actions that you can take to accomplish each goal.

2. Set up your calendars for the year. Mark each month and dates for the next 12 months.

3. Populate any important dates that you know off the top of your head. Think of any major events that have happened recently. Are there anniversaries or birthdays that you want to mark to remember? If your mind is blank, no worries. Just fill them in as you remember.

4. Keep your eyes open to those who are hurting throughout the month. Write down the names of those who are put on your heart to help. Think of things you can do to help them and write them down. As you write them down, add any important dates you need to remember to the calendars.

5. Don't forget to keep referring to your Comfort Zone! You did the work of finding what works for you, so put it to use!

6. Keep track of your marbles! For each comfort connections that you make, check a number off the list. They all add up and as you see your numbers rise, you will feel that circle of comfort in action.

7. Recap the month with your highs and lows.

Don't worry if you don't hit all your goals, even hitting some of them will help create a culture of comfort that can help mend our divided world. But rest assured if you continue to focus on this it will become a natural part of your daily life.

Note: We know many of you are used to using online tools – but we have you assess and create your comfort plan manually because science has shown the power of the written word. It's better for learning, keeps you from being distracted and allows you to be off your screens.

If you could only sense how important you are to the lives of those you meet; how important you can be to the people you may never even dream of. There is something of yourself that you leave at every meeting with another person.

~ *FRED ROGERS*

RECAPPING YOUR COMFORT PROFILE

MY AWKWARD IS THIS

The three least relatable comfort dog traits: (pg. 192)

1. _____
2. _____
3. _____

My biggest barriers to comforting others: (pg. 193)

1. _____
2. _____
3. _____

My supermarket scenario relatable responses: (pg. 194)

1. _____
2. _____
3. _____

My three lowest scoring comfort strengths: (pg. 194)

1. _____
2. _____
3. _____

Ears / Listening - (pg. 197)
If you circled boxes 3 or 4 write the words here

Eyes / Seeing - If you circled boxes 3 or 4
write the words here

If you wrote an answer above in ears or eyes, please recognize you will need
to shift your mindset and practice and develop strategies to improve your
listening/seeing.

Five awkward phrases I need to avoid: (pg. 196)

1. _____
2. _____
3. _____
4. _____
5. _____

My two least favorite ways of writing comfort: (pg. 198)

1. _____
2. _____

My five lowest scoring gifts of action (pg. 198)

1. _____
2. _____
3. _____
4. _____
5. _____

My least favorite age groups to work with (pg. 199)

1. _____
2. _____

My 3 least favorite ways to communicate: (pg. 199)

1. _____
2. _____
3. _____

MY COMFORT ZONE IS THIS

The three most relatable comfort dog traits: (pg.192)

1. _____
2. _____
3. _____

Three trends that I care about: (pg.192)

1. _____
2. _____
3. _____

Three statistics that concern me: (pg.192)

1. _____
2. _____
3. _____

My top words of comfort and my comfort phrase: (pg.193)

_____

_____

Areas where I feel most equipped and/or motivated to help: (pg.195)

1. _____
2. _____
3. _____
4. _____
5. _____

My three highest scoring comfort strengths: (pg.194)

1. _____
2. _____
3. _____

Ears / Listening – If you circled boxes 1 or 2 write the words here

Eyes / Seeing – If you circled boxes 1 or 2 write the words here

Five comfort phrases that resonate with me (pg.196)

1. _____
2. _____
3. _____
4. _____
5. _____

My favorite ways of writing comfort: (pg.198)

1. _____
2. _____

My five highest scoring gifts of action (pg.198)

1. _____
2. _____
3. _____
4. _____
5. _____

My favorite age groups to work with (pg.198)

1. _____
2. _____

My three favorite ways to communicate: (pg.198)

1. _____
2. _____
3. _____

Comfort action items that resonate with me and I would enjoy doing: (pg.198)

1. _____
2. _____
3. _____

(pg.200)

How many hours of distraction per week did I identify:_____

What three days/time each week are windows of opportunity to reach out to those who need my support and comfort?

DAY _____   TIME _____

DAY _____   TIME _____

DAY _____   TIME _____

COMFORT ACTION PLAN: JANUARY

My personal comfort goals and achievements for this month

MY COMFORT ZONE GOALS
- ☐ _____
- ☐ _____
- ☐ _____
- ☐ _____
- ☐ _____

MY AWKWARD ZONE GOALS
- ☐ _____
- ☐ _____
- ☐ _____
- ☐ _____
- ☐ _____

WHO I CAN COMFORT THIS MONTH

NAME	WHY/ WHAT DO THEY NEED

MARBLE TRACKER
check off one for each
meaningful connection

○ ○ ○ ○ ○ ○ ○
○ ○ ○ ○ ○ ○ ○
○ ○ ○ ○ ○ ○ ○
○ ○ ○ ○ ○ ○ ○
○ ○ ○ ○ ○ ○ ○
○ ○ ○ ○ ○ ○ ○

THINGS THAT WORKED THIS MONTH
_____
_____
_____
_____

THINGS I CAN WORK ON NEXT MONTH
_____
_____
_____
_____

COMFORT ACTION PLAN: FEBRUARY

My personal comfort goals and achievements for this month

MY COMFORT ZONE GOALS

- [ ] _____
- [ ] _____
- [ ] _____
- [ ] _____
- [ ] _____

MY AWKWARD ZONE GOALS

- [ ] _____
- [ ] _____
- [ ] _____
- [ ] _____
- [ ] _____

WHO I CAN COMFORT THIS MONTH

NAME	WHY/ WHAT DO THEY NEED

MARBLE TRACKER

check off one for each
meaningful connection

○ ○ ○ ○ ○ ○ ○
○ ○ ○ ○ ○ ○ ○
○ ○ ○ ○ ○ ○ ○
○ ○ ○ ○ ○ ○ ○
○ ○ ○ ○ ○ ○ ○
○ ○ ○ ○ ○ ○ ○

THINGS THAT WORKED THIS MONTH

_____
_____
_____
_____

THINGS I CAN WORK ON NEXT MONTH

_____
_____
_____
_____

COMFORT ACTION PLAN: MARCH

My personal comfort goals and achievements for this month

MY COMFORT ZONE GOALS

- [ ] ....
- [ ] ....
- [ ] ....
- [ ] ....
- [ ] ....

MY AWKWARD ZONE GOALS

- [ ] ....
- [ ] ....
- [ ] ....
- [ ] ....
- [ ] ....

WHO I CAN COMFORT THIS MONTH

NAME

WHY/ WHAT DO THEY NEED

MARBLE TRACKER

check off one for each
meaningful connection

○ ○ ○ ○ ○ ○ ○ ○
○ ○ ○ ○ ○ ○ ○ ○
○ ○ ○ ○ ○ ○ ○ ○
○ ○ ○ ○ ○ ○ ○ ○
○ ○ ○ ○ ○ ○ ○ ○
○ ○ ○ ○ ○ ○ ○ ○

THINGS THAT WORKED THIS MONTH

_____

_____

_____

THINGS I CAN WORK ON NEXT MONTH

_____

_____

_____

COMFORT ACTION PLAN: APRIL

My personal comfort goals and achievements for this month

MY COMFORT ZONE GOALS

- ☐ _____
- ☐ _____
- ☐ _____
- ☐ _____
- ☐ _____

MY AWKWARD ZONE GOALS

- ☐ _____
- ☐ _____
- ☐ _____
- ☐ _____
- ☐ _____

WHO I CAN COMFORT THIS MONTH

NAME   **WHY/ WHAT DO THEY NEED**

MARBLE TRACKER

check off one for each
meaningful connection

○ ○ ○ ○ ○ ○ ○ ○
○ ○ ○ ○ ○ ○ ○ ○
○ ○ ○ ○ ○ ○ ○ ○
○ ○ ○ ○ ○ ○ ○ ○
○ ○ ○ ○ ○ ○ ○ ○
○ ○ ○ ○ ○ ○ ○ ○
○ ○ ○ ○ ○ ○ ○ ○

THINGS THAT WORKED THIS MONTH

_____
_____
_____
_____

THINGS I CAN WORK ON NEXT MONTH

_____
_____
_____
_____

COMFORT ACTION PLAN: MAY

My personal comfort goals and achievements for this month

MY COMFORT ZONE GOALS
☐ _____
☐ _____
☐ _____
☐ _____
☐ _____

MY AWKWARD ZONE GOALS
☐ _____
☐ _____
☐ _____
☐ _____
☐ _____

WHO I CAN COMFORT THIS MONTH

NAME   **WHY/ WHAT DO THEY NEED**

MARBLE TRACKER
check off one for each
meaningful connection

○ ○ ○ ○ ○ ○ ○
○ ○ ○ ○ ○ ○ ○
○ ○ ○ ○ ○ ○ ○
○ ○ ○ ○ ○ ○ ○
○ ○ ○ ○ ○ ○ ○
○ ○ ○ ○ ○ ○ ○

THINGS THAT WORKED THIS MONTH

_____
_____
_____
_____

THINGS I CAN WORK ON NEXT MONTH

_____
_____
_____
_____

COMFORT ACTION PLAN: JUNE

My personal comfort goals and achievements for this month

MY COMFORT ZONE GOALS

- ☐ _____
- ☐ _____
- ☐ _____
- ☐ _____
- ☐ _____

MY AWKWARD ZONE GOALS

- ☐ _____
- ☐ _____
- ☐ _____
- ☐ _____
- ☐ _____

WHO I CAN COMFORT THIS MONTH

NAME   WHY/ WHAT DO THEY NEED

MARBLE TRACKER

check off one for each
meaningful connection

○ ○ ○ ○ ○ ○ ○
○ ○ ○ ○ ○ ○ ○
○ ○ ○ ○ ○ ○ ○
○ ○ ○ ○ ○ ○ ○
○ ○ ○ ○ ○ ○ ○
○ ○ ○ ○ ○ ○ ○
○ ○ ○ ○ ○ ○ ○

THINGS THAT WORKED THIS MONTH

_____
_____
_____
_____

THINGS I CAN WORK ON NEXT MONTH

_____
_____
_____
_____

COMFORT ACTION PLAN: JULY

My personal comfort goals and achievements for this month

MY COMFORT ZONE GOALS

- ☐ _____
- ☐ _____
- ☐ _____
- ☐ _____
- ☐ _____

MY AWKWARD ZONE GOALS

- ☐ _____
- ☐ _____
- ☐ _____
- ☐ _____
- ☐ _____

WHO I CAN COMFORT THIS MONTH

NAME   **WHY/ WHAT DO THEY NEED**

MARBLE TRACKER
check off one for each
meaningful connection

○ ○ ○ ○ ○ ○ ○
○ ○ ○ ○ ○ ○ ○
○ ○ ○ ○ ○ ○ ○
○ ○ ○ ○ ○ ○ ○
○ ○ ○ ○ ○ ○ ○
○ ○ ○ ○ ○ ○ ○

THINGS THAT WORKED THIS MONTH

_____
_____
_____
_____

THINGS I CAN WORK ON NEXT MONTH

_____
_____
_____
_____

COMFORT ACTION PLAN: AUGUST

My personal comfort goals and achievements for this month

MY COMFORT ZONE GOALS

- ☐ _____
- ☐ _____
- ☐ _____
- ☐ _____
- ☐ _____

MY AWKWARD ZONE GOALS

- ☐ _____
- ☐ _____
- ☐ _____
- ☐ _____
- ☐ _____

WHO I CAN COMFORT THIS MONTH

NAME	WHY/ WHAT DO THEY NEED

MARBLE TRACKER

check off one for each
meaningful connection

○ ○ ○ ○ ○ ○
○ ○ ○ ○ ○ ○
○ ○ ○ ○ ○ ○
○ ○ ○ ○ ○ ○
○ ○ ○ ○ ○ ○
○ ○ ○ ○ ○ ○

THINGS THAT WORKED THIS MONTH

_____
_____
_____
_____

THINGS I CAN WORK ON NEXT MONTH

_____
_____
_____
_____

COMFORT ACTION PLAN: SEPTEMBER

My personal comfort goals and achievements for this month

MY COMFORT ZONE GOALS

- ☐ _____
- ☐ _____
- ☐ _____
- ☐ _____
- ☐ _____

MY AWKWARD ZONE GOALS

- ☐ _____
- ☐ _____
- ☐ _____
- ☐ _____
- ☐ _____

WHO I CAN COMFORT THIS MONTH

NAME **WHY/ WHAT DO THEY NEED**

MARBLE TRACKER
check off one for each
meaningful connection

○ ○ ○ ○ ○ ○ ○ ○
○ ○ ○ ○ ○ ○ ○ ○
○ ○ ○ ○ ○ ○ ○ ○
○ ○ ○ ○ ○ ○ ○ ○
○ ○ ○ ○ ○ ○ ○ ○
○ ○ ○ ○ ○ ○ ○ ○

THINGS THAT WORKED THIS MONTH

_____
_____
_____
_____

THINGS I CAN WORK ON NEXT MONTH

_____
_____
_____
_____

COMFORT ACTION PLAN: OCTOBER

My personal comfort goals and achievements for this month

MY COMFORT ZONE GOALS

- [ ] _____
- [ ] _____
- [ ] _____
- [ ] _____
- [ ] _____

MY AWKWARD ZONE GOALS

- [ ] _____
- [ ] _____
- [ ] _____
- [ ] _____
- [ ] _____

WHO I CAN COMFORT THIS MONTH

NAME	WHY/ WHAT DO THEY NEED

MARBLE TRACKER

check off one for each
meaningful connection

○ ○ ○ ○ ○ ○ ○
○ ○ ○ ○ ○ ○ ○
○ ○ ○ ○ ○ ○ ○
○ ○ ○ ○ ○ ○ ○
○ ○ ○ ○ ○ ○ ○
○ ○ ○ ○ ○ ○ ○

THINGS THAT WORKED THIS MONTH

_____
_____
_____
_____

THINGS I CAN WORK ON NEXT MONTH

_____
_____
_____
_____

COMFORT ACTION PLAN: NOVEMBER

My personal comfort goals and achievements for this month

MY COMFORT ZONE GOALS

- ☐ _____
- ☐ _____
- ☐ _____
- ☐ _____
- ☐ _____

MY AWKWARD ZONE GOALS

- ☐ _____
- ☐ _____
- ☐ _____
- ☐ _____
- ☐ _____

WHO I CAN COMFORT THIS MONTH

NAME   **WHY/ WHAT DO THEY NEED**

MARBLE TRACKER

check off one for each
meaningful connection

○ ○ ○ ○ ○ ○ ○ ○
○ ○ ○ ○ ○ ○ ○ ○
○ ○ ○ ○ ○ ○ ○ ○
○ ○ ○ ○ ○ ○ ○ ○
○ ○ ○ ○ ○ ○ ○ ○
○ ○ ○ ○ ○ ○ ○ ○

THINGS THAT WORKED THIS MONTH

_____
_____
_____

THINGS I CAN WORK ON NEXT MONTH

_____
_____
_____

COMFORT ACTION PLAN: DECEMBER

My personal comfort goals and achievements for this month

MY COMFORT ZONE GOALS

- ☐ _____
- ☐ _____
- ☐ _____
- ☐ _____
- ☐ _____

MY AWKWARD ZONE GOALS

- ☐ _____
- ☐ _____
- ☐ _____
- ☐ _____
- ☐ _____

WHO I CAN COMFORT THIS MONTH

NAME	WHY/ WHAT DO THEY NEED

MARBLE TRACKER

check off one for each
meaningful connection

○ ○ ○ ○ ○ ○ ○ ○
○ ○ ○ ○ ○ ○ ○ ○
○ ○ ○ ○ ○ ○ ○ ○
○ ○ ○ ○ ○ ○ ○ ○
○ ○ ○ ○ ○ ○ ○ ○
○ ○ ○ ○ ○ ○ ○ ○

THINGS THAT WORKED THIS MONTH

_____
_____
_____
_____

THINGS I CAN WORK ON NEXT MONTH

_____
_____
_____
_____

FINAL THOUGHTS

Dear Friends,

There has never been a time such as this in our history. Our world is changing, and it is calling for your help. The way our society currently treats and cares for each other isn't working, we are losing our way. As simple as the concept sounds, we need to relearn the powerful skill of comfort that we were all born with. We need to help mend our disconnected world.

You may have found the trends and statistics I presented disheartening and maybe they are. However I prefer to look at the time we are in as an opportunity. There is a need and you can now be part of the solution. Even better, it's a solution that can add deep meaning and purpose in your own life. For it's in helping others where we make a difference. When we make a difference, we feel empowered and when we feel empowered we feel purpose.

People who need comfort carry many difficult emotions – anxiety, hopelessness, fear, guilt, loneliness, depression, anger, envy and bitterness as a start. They can be a new different version of the person you know. This can be hard to face. You don't know how to respond. It's awkward.

But we at Inspiring Comfort are finding that the best remedy for these difficult emotions is for a friend to find them, for comfort to find them, for love to find them.

You can be the one that finds them. You can be the comfort that brings some light and love to someone feeling only dark.

It is my deepest hope and sincerest desire that the strategies and tools in this book will help you overcome the awkwardness that stops us from seeing those in need. The love and comfort you pour out **will** come back to you.
This I can promise.

The need is great. The circle of comfort is real. You are equipped. You are needed. You are able.

Go and find them. Be that love.

With Comfort & Hope,

WITH GRATITUDE

How can I thank all of the extraordinary people who pushed me through my Awkward Zone and allowed this book to be? Seems impossible but let me try.

To my family:
- Erika, Ashlyn and Audrey - For your incredible love, support and understanding of the passion I have for this work. For each missed minute of being together because of it and for knowing when to comfort me when I need it. You have my heart. Always and forever.
- My parents Dave & Betty - For raising me to know in the depth of my soul what it takes to care for and comfort each other. If everyone in the world lived like you do, there would be no need for this book.
- My sisters Julie & Renata who walked me through my every writing terror and calmed my nerves. Who have led me to an even deeper understanding of faith, care and support as we navigate the waters of losing dear Tom.
- My personal teachers of comfort – Shelby & Cali – woof.

The Comfort Team:
- To Skye – For bringing the vision of this book to life far beyond my wildest dreams, what can I even say? I'm still not sure what I ever did to deserve the incredible you. Thank you seems so inadequate.
- To Mary – For being at my side talking through every idea and strategy as we dragged suitcases across the country with our supplies and tested every lesson and for praying our way to where we are today. This comfort journey simply would not be if it were not for you.
- To Jill –For being my fabulous friend far before comfort was even on my radar and for teaching me tenacity as we ran together. For joining our comfort journey at the most perfect time and allowing us to grow and thrive. You are the ying to my yang.
- To Jeff & Ken - for allowing your amazing wives to walk this road with me and even helping to chart our course along the way. Your support, encouragement and wisdom are the best bonus gifts of all.
- Kelly & Byron – Best. Interns. Ever.
- Brian, Laurel, Mateusz, Eric, Sean, Kristen, Josh, Steve & the team at New Degree Press: For bringing the vision, structure, guidance and support to do the impossible: Dream up, research, write, promote, fund, design, edit, print and distribute a book in 10 months. Just wow.
- Contributors to the book: For gracing us with your beautiful words and sharing your stories: Lisa Procaccini, Betty Reul, Julie Wall, Christa Carone, Laura Mayer, Daniel Mattila, Byron Bushara, Kelly Shannon, Kim & Ellie Bepko, Betsy Krauss, Barb & Paige Tarpey, Bill & Adriann Nelson, Graig Greenlee and Ellen Strommen
- For bringing science to the skill: Dr. David DeSteno, Dr. Lynn Allen, Dr. Gabe Lomas, Dr. John Draper,

Who have played a role in making this book possible:
- The original comfort crew, the roots of this book were formed together with you in Danbury CT: Bill, Tom & Nancy, Wendy, Lois, Anneliese, Joel, Jan, Cynthia, Deb, Deana, Lisa, Diane, Cindy, Kathryn, Lil.
- The staff & teachers of Sandy Hook School – I carry your pain on my heart every single day. It is what has fueled so much of my passion for this book. I will never forget. #HOTWIG
- Early Believers in Comfort; Jeanene for spray painting our first 500 plaques by hand and Liz, Jill, Helayna, Stacy, Sheri, Jane, Dawn and Sue for spreading our first ripples of comfort.
- The Lutheran Church Charities K-9 Comfort Dog team & family – for sharing the mercy, compassion, presence and proclamation of Jesus Christ to those who are suffering and in need.
- Pastors Tyson, Mann, Harper and Froehlich for your spiritual guidance and support.
- John Maxwell and the JMT DNA
- For believing in the mission of comfort: Don, Carolyn, Ed, Michelle Weidenbrenner, Beth Comstock, Joseph Aoun, Helen Vollmer.

Kickstarter Gratitude

We are grateful for the amazing support from the following individuals who believe in us and our mission of comfort.

Leaders Of Comfort

Chris and Paul Schwan, David Marr, Geoff Beattie and Amanda Lang, George and Jodi Folta, Jeff and Jill Bornstein, Jeff and Andy Immelt, Jessica and John Wood, John Fish, Matt and Nicole Cribbins

Growers of Comfort

Alex and Jill Dimitrief, Dave and Nicole Nason, Deb and Mark Boedicker, Domenica de Fazio, Elaine Cox, Harry Dhaliwal, Jeanene Wedertz Hupy, Jerry and Sharon Garavel, Joe and Debbie Mirra, Judith Gladden, Keith and Janet Sherin, John and Lori Berisford, Margaret Wade, Marilyn Parke, Michael and Julie Bradley, Paula Daher, Puneet Mahajan, Rachelle Glyman, Robert and Veronica Green, Trevor and Kyle Schauenberg, Warren and Linda Marr, William Cohan

Core Comforters

AJ Romeo, Allison Stockel, Andrea Jones, Brackett Denniston, Brenda Berta, Chip and Kathy Froehlich, Chris Gale, Daniel & Diane Parrilli, Dawn Gilfry, Deborah Fahncke, Delaine Mazich, Elisabeth Ruscitti, Elizabeth Cummings, Ellen Strommen, Joan Myer, Jeff Butchen, Jim and Tracy Duddy, Jim Follett, John Keundig, Jonathan and Cindy Chase, Julie and Steve Wall, Julie Ann Green, Kat Bunker, Kathy Lang, Kevin McGrath and Robin Copeland, Khozema Shipchandler, Kim Bishop, Kim Marshall, Lance Gurney, Laura Rotegard, LeAnn Rogers, Lee Cooper, LeRoy and Carol Crocker, Libby Robertson, Liz Riggs, Lynda and Jack Withiam, Lynn Allen, Margaret Hajdarovic, Mary Perry, Matthew Susser, Michael and Maria Flynn, Mike Fisher, Nelson Family, Nicole Abbatecola, Pamela Christensen, Pat Breux, Patricia Sumner, Paul Bucci, Renata and David Bowers, Ridgefield Academy, Riley John, Stephen and Judith Scala, Sue Johnson, Susan Hartong, Tom and Merni Libonate, Vera Manoukian, William Harford

Comfort Supporters

Abigail Kagan, Adrienne Muraski Landgrave, Alan and Donna Spose, Alan Korobkin, Alex Bornstein, Allison Bernhardt, Allison Kraft, Amanda Vedder, Amy Jones, Amy Zietlow, Andrew Bornstein, Andrew Knight, Aneeka Britto, Anissa DeMatteo, Ann Cleaver, Ann J. Marr, Ann Margaret Mannix, Ann McGrath, Anne Giordano, Anne Klis, Annie Landgrave, Ashlyn Marr,

Barb Granado, Barbara Flaum, Barbara Furlo, Barbara Lewis, Barbara Sullivan, Becky Cleason, Becky McIlwain, Beth Comstock, Beth Munnelly, Beth Pajak, Betsy Brand, Betsy Fitzpatrick, Betsy Krauss, Beverly Neal, Beverly Becker, Bonnie Boldt, Bonnie Wanzer, Brenda McElroy, Brian Hajdarovic, Bridget Miller, Camille Dareau, Carl Kuehner, Caroline Suvcott, Catherine Dunleavy, Catherine Scatterday, Cathy Snopkowski, Catie Sinden-Stolte, Charlene Conklin, Charn Konrath, Chrissy Dunleavy, Christa Carone, Christina Packard, Christine Carnicelli, Christine Groth, Christine Hruska, Christine Yergler, Christy Hatcher, Cindy Ciccia, Cindy Lentol, Claire Roehl, Clay Snyder, Colleen Cugine, Colleen McGough, Cynthia Flood, Diane Froelick, Dan Colao, Dan Marr, Danielle Beylouni Cone, Darlene Worischeck, Dave and Betty Reul, Dave Woodward, David van Wees, Deb Erdmann, Deb Povinelli, Debbie Hesse, Debbie Uhlhorn Dietrich, Debi Cruger, Deborah Starke Justice, Diana Bunt, Diane Ahern, Diane McNamara, Diane Parson, Diane Sinitsky, Donna Davis, Dot Mock, Dottie Simonides, Dunbar Okeson, Ed DeCosta, Edith Gengras, Eileen Cunningham, Eileen Snoddy, Elizabeth Isaacson, Elizabeth Porter, Elizabeth Side, Ellen and Lance Gurney, Ellen Balge, Ellen Matthews, Emily Perry, Emmanuel Lanzo, Emmy Starr, Eric and Courtney Stadelmann, Eric Koester, Erika Johanek, Erika Marr, Erin Mcgarry, Gael Lynch, Gary Scheffer, Gayle Leonard, Geoffrey Miller, Gill Rogers, Gina M. McAveeney, Gina Seward, Glori Norwitt, Gretchen McMahon, Haley Boesky, Haley Koch, Helayna Pace, James Richards, Jackie and Scott Scholten, Jacque Lang, Jan Dearth, Jan Hauser, Jane Marsh-Johnson, Jane Peterson, Janet Boyer, Janet Halpin, Janice Semper, Janice Wissert, Jason St. Onge, Jeanette Horan, Jeffrey Ford, Jenipher Lagana, Jennifer Lundberg, Jennifer Englert, Jennifer Giordano, Jennifer Mark, Jessica Branson, Jill Zempel, Jim and Lisa Carroll, Jim Ziolkowski, Joan Kannegieser, Joe Crocker, JoEllen McIntire, John Azzilonna, John Kearns, John Panning, John Rice, Jonathan Schultz, Joseh Heinzmann, Joseph Aoun, Joseph Ciccia, Joseph M. Pastore III, Joshua Morgan, Joyce Bordash, Joyce Sarver, Joyce R. Sauca, JP Mikhael, Julie Blyckert, Julie Garrison, Julie Hughes, Julie Leff, Julie Schwartz, Julie Weede, Kaitlyn Hayes, Kara Rillings Morgan, Karen Fulkerson, Karen Henrie, Karen Torstenson, Karen Voss Sardone, Karla Murtaugh, Kate Turner, Kathie Brennan, Kathleen Doyle-Kelly, Kathryn A. Cassidy, Kathryn Christofferson, Kathy Reuter, Kathy Smith, Katie Thomson, Kay Lewis, Keller Arnold, Kelly Runyan, Kelsey Marr, Ken Perry, Kim Bepko, Kim Spencer, Kelly McCarthy, Kori Stolte DeSio, Kris Feda, Kristen Duckett, Kristen Hoban, Kristen Weber, Kristin Beylouni, Kristin Briggs, Kristin Lawless, Kristin Whitney-DeLeo, Kyra and Rudy Carbone, Larry and Susan Ring, Laura Dobson, Laura M. Feinstein, Laura Mayer, Laura Elizabeth Hamner, Lauren Marr, Laurie DeFrancesco, Laurie DoBosh, Lenore Welsh, Linda Cameron, Linda Cinquegrana, Linda Hatcher, Linda Merkle, Lindsey Seitz, Lisa Bisceglia, Lisa Haden, Lisa P. Elsberry, Lisa Rizzari, Lisa Smith, Lois Weiss, Lori Anrico, Lori Arute, Lori Luetzow, Lori Woodruff, Lorna Szalay, LuAnn Kelly, LuAnne Flom, Lynne Autorino, Lynn Buhrke, Malcolm MacGregor, Mara Sullivan, Marc Friedman, Marcella Kunstek, Marci Tregurtha, Marcie Coffin, Marcie Maguire, Maria Onorato, Marilyn Chandley, Marilyn Hamilton, Marilyn Woods, Martha Amstutz, Martie Dunnett, Mary Ann Jacob, Mary Burch, Mary Jean Heller, Mary Kay Sloan, Mary Ludlum, Mary Lux, Mary Todd, Matt Bornstein, Matthew Roche, Maura Gidez Kilner, Maureen Johnson, Max Bornstein, Megan Blackstone Searfoss, Meredith Rogers, Michael Vinick, Michele Arnold, Michelle Weidenbrenner, Mike Marrinan, Nan Lally, Nan Merolla, Napoleon Monroe, Natalie Rogers, Ned Waterhouse, Niamh Diorio, Nick Rinaldi, Nicole Connors, Nicole Kovensky, Nikki Deacon, Olive Kristine Howe, Pamela Lancaster, Pamela Tanenbaum, Patricia Patterson, Patti Milazzo, Patti Ross, Paula Mariner, Paula Price, Peggy Wilson, Pete and Kim Tarnapoll, Peter Flink, Peter Foss, Peter Spambanato, Polly Edwards, Ralph Buchhorn, Randy and Rose Salazar, Regina Benjamin, Rick Pollock, Robert Dolan, Robert Perry, Robert Trainer, Robin Powell, Robin Walker, Ron Hynes, Rory Ahearn, Rose Jallits, Ruth Padgett, Ryan Pliner, Sally Lewis, Sandra Smith, Sandy Shavlik, Scott Usher, Sean Dowd, Sean McEvoy, Shar Farran, Sharon Signorelli, Shawn McAteer, Sheryl Bates, Simonne Hewett, Spencer Gehring, Stacey Bradford, Stacey Carney, Stacy Hynes, Stephanie Astell, Sue Roth Samiljan, Susan Feeser, Susan Holland, Susan J. Groth, Susan Ragonetti, Susan Yergler, Susan Zimmerman, Suzanne and John Kluge, Suzanne Bellagama Brennan, Suzanne Raffalli, Suzie Meierdierks, Teddy Berlin, Tehri Gasparrini, Teresa Waldron, Terra Henson, Terri Gibbons, Terri Janki, Terry Bruner, Tess Denton, The Stewart Family, Tiffany McMahon, Tim Daubenspeck, Toby Soli, Tom Reynolds, Tom St Onge, Tom Weber, Toni Bazon, Tracy Fincher, Tracy Hunt, Tracy Warren, Tricia Brody, Trisha Olinger Rountree, Trudy Hakala, Tyler Koch, Tyson Labuhn, Valerie van Beek, Vicky Paullin Wolfe, Victor Williams, Victoria Dinkel, Vincent Polito, Wendy Cole, Wendy Killeen, Whitney Callan, William "Mo" Cowan, William McGimpsey, William Sinnott, Yvonne Putz

SOURCES BY CHAPTER

#3 How Do Dogs Do That

Human Animal Bond Research Institute, "Survey: Pet Owners and the Human-Animal Bond," accessed April 19, 2019, https://habri.org/2016-pet-owners-survey

Steven Feldman, "For Better Mental Health, Experience the Pet Effect," Mental Health America, accessed April 21, 2019, http://www.mentalhealthamerica.net/blog/better-mental-health-experience-pet-effect

Sharon Maguire, "Understanding a Dog's Senses," Dog Breed Info Center, accessed April 22, 2019, https://www.dogbreedinfo.com/articles/dog-senses.htm

Marissa Leotaud, "Can Dogs Smell Our Emotions?", Cuteness, accessed April 22, 2019, https://www.cuteness.com/13712832/can-dogs-smell-our-emotions

VetInfo, "Dog Communication: How Dogs Talk to Humans and Each Other," accessed April 22, 2019, https://www.vetinfo/dog-communication.html

Amy Shojai, "Understanding Dog Talk," The Spruce Pets, accessed April 22, 2019, https://www.thesprucepets.com/dog-language-understanding-dog-talk-2804565

Animal Planet, "Why Do Dogs Wag Their Tails?", accessed April 23, 2019, http://www.animalplanet.com/pets/why-do-dogs-wag-their-tails/

David A. Keeps, "The Science Behind How Dogs Make Us Happier, Healthier, and Fitter," Men's Journal, accessed April 23, 2019, https://www.mensjournal.com/health-fitness/the-science-behind-how-dogs-make-us-happier-healthier-and-fitter-w431916/

#7 Why Are We Losing Our Way

Dan Diamond, "Mass Shootings Are Rising. Here's How To Stop Them.", Forbes, accessed May 1, 2019, https://www.forbes.com/sites/dandiamond/2015/06/18/charleston-deaths-are-an-american-tragedy-mass-shootings-are-rising/#61f14bf9787b

Anne-Marie Botek, "Combatting the Epidemic of Loneliness in Seniors," AgingCare, accessed April 24, 2019, https://www.agingcare.com/articles/loneliness-in-the-elderly-151549.htm

Bob Woods, "America's $103 billion home health-care system is in crisis as worker shortage worsens," CNBC, accessed April 19, 2019, https://www.cnbc.com/2019/04/09/us-home-healthcare-system-is-in-crisis-as-worker-shortages-worsen.html

Jonathan Coppage, "Kids are living with their parents longer. It's a good thing.", The Washington Post, accessed April 11, 2019, https://www.washingtonpost.com/opinions/kids-are-living-with-their-parents-longer-its-a-good-thing/2017/07/07/e171d346-625b-11e7-a4f7-af-34fc1d9d39_story.html (https://www.washingtonpost.com/opinions/kids-are-living-with-their-parents-longer-its-a-good-thing/2017/07/07/e171d346-625b-11e7-a4f7-af34fc1d9d39_story.html?utm_term=.d843b21def32)

Jane Barratt, "We are living longer than ever. But are we living better?", STAT, accessed April 24, 2019, https://www.statnews.com/2017/02/14/living-longer-living-better-aging/

Institute of Medicine (US) Committee on Implications of For-Profit Enterprise in Health Care; Gray BH, editor. For-Profit Enterprise in Health Care. Washington (DC): National Academies Press (US); 1986. The Changing Structure of the Nursing Home Industry and the Impact of Ownership on Quality, Cost, and Access. Available from: https://www.ncbi.nlm.nih.gov/books/NBK217907/

Catherine Hawes and Charles D. Phillips, "The Changing Structure of the Nursing Home Industry and the Impact of Ownership on Quality, Cost, and Access," National Academies Press (1986), https://www.ncbi.nlm.nih.gov/books/NBK217907/

Sophie Bethune & Elizabeth Lewan, "Stress About Health Insurance Costs Reported By Majority of Americans, APA Stress in America Survey Reveals," American Psychological Association, accessed April 19, 2019, https://www.apa.org/news/press/releases/2018/01/insurance-costs

Michaeleen Doucleff, "We're Living Longer, But Not All That Healthier," NPR, accessed April 22, 2019, https://www.npr.org/sections/health-shots/2012/12/12/167122571/were-living-longer-but-not-all-that-healthier

Alina Surís, Ryan Holliday, & Carol S. North, The Evolution of the Classification of Psychiatric Disorders, Behavioral Sciences, 6(1), 5 (2016). doi:10.3390/bs6010005

Patrick L. Remington MD & Ross C. Brownson, PhD, "Fifty Years of Progress in Chronic Disease Epidemiology and Control," Centers for Disease Control and Prevention, accessed April 22, 2019, https://www.cdc.gov/mmwr/preview/mmwrhtml/su6004a12.htm

Niraj Chokshi, "Americans Are Among the Most Stressed People in the World, Poll Finds," The New York Times, accessed April 25, 2019, https://www.nytimes.com/2019/04/25/us/americans-stressful.html

Thomas G. Plante, Ph.D, "Americans Are Stressed Out, and It Is Getting Worse," Psychology Today, accessed April 25, 2019, https://www.psychologytoday.com/us/blog/do-the-right-thing/201812/americans-are-stressed-out-and-it-is-getting-worse

Rabah Kamal & Cynthia Cox, "How has U.S. spending on healthcare changed over time?" Peterson-Kaiser Health System Tracker, accessed April 26, 2019, https://www.healthsystemtracker.org/chart-collection/u-s-spending-health-care-changed-time/#item-start

Monique Ellis, "The top 10 medical advances in history," Proclinical, accessed April 27, 2019, https://www.proclinical.com/blogs/2017-11/the-top-10-medical-advances-in-history

Infoplease, "US Household and Family Statistics," accessed June 1, 2019, https://www.infoplease.com/us/household-and-family-statistics/us-households-size-1790-2006

Answers.Com, "When Did Computers Become Popular," accessed April 20, 2019, https://www.answers.com/Q/When_did_computers_become_popular

Pew Research Center, "Mobile Fact Sheet," accessed June 12, 2019, https://www.pewinternet.org/fact-sheet/mobile/

Kenneth Burke, "How Many Texts Do People Send Every Day (2018)?", Text Request, accessed April 14, 2019, https://www.textrequest.com/blog/how-many-texts-people-send-per-day/

iTalk, "A Brief History of the Home Telephone," accessed April 15, 2019, https://www.italktelecom.co.uk/blog/a-brief-history-of-the-home-telephone

Craig Smith, "145 Snapchat Statistics, Facts, and Figures [2019]," Expanded Ramblings, accessed September 6, 2019, https://expandedramblings.com/index.php/snapchat-statistics/

Nick O'Neill, "Google Now Indexes 620 Million Facebook Groups," Adweek, LLC, accessed June 10, 2019, https://www.adweek.com/digital/google-now-indexes-620-million-facebook-groups/

Statistica, "Number of monthly active Facebook users worldwide as of 2nd quarter 2019 (in millions)," accessed June 10, 2019, https://www.statista.com/statistics/264810/number-of-monthly-active-facebook-users-worldwide/

The Associated Press, "Number of active users at Facebook over the years," Yahoo! Finance, accessed June 10, 2019, https://finance.yahoo.com/news/number-active-users-facebook-over-years-214600186--finance.html

Chayenne Polimédio, Church Attendance and the Decline of Civic Spaces, Pacific Standard, accessed April 27, 2019, https://psmag.com/social-justice/losing-our-religion-and-its-spaces

Wikipedia, "Modernization theory," accessed April 27, 2019, https://en.wikipedia.org/wiki/Modernization_theory

Scott Cook, "The Decline of the American Front Porch," Virginia.Edu, accessed April 27, 2019, http://xroads.virginia.edu/~CLASS/am483_97/projects/cook/decline.htm

Robert Putnam, "The Strange Disappearance of Civic America," The American Prospect, accessed April 28, 2019, https://prospect.org/article/strange-disappearance-civic-america

John T. Cacioppo, Ph.D, "It's Time for a Science of Social Connection," Psychology Today, accessed April 28, 2019, https://www.psychologytoday.com/us/blog/connections/201007/its-time-science-social-connection

Alan Kandel, "Fifty years of American commuting – 1960-2009: What the numbers say," Air Quality Matters (blog), Scienceblog, June 15, 2013, https://al-ankandel.scienceblog.com/2013/06/15/fifty-years-of-american-commuting-1960-2009-what-the-numbers-say/

Molly Fischer, "What Happens When Work Becomes a Nonstop Chat Room," NYMag, accessed April 27, 2019, http://nymag.com/intelligencer/2017/05/what-has-slack-done-to-the-office.html

The United States Census Bureau, "High School Completion Rate Is Highest in U.S. History," accessed May 1, 2019, https://www.census.gov/newsroom/press-releases/2017/educational-attainment-2017.html

Jana Riess, "Religion declining in importance for many Americans, especially for Millennials," Religion News, accessed May 2, 2019, https://religionnews.com/2018/12/10/religion-declining-in-importance-for-many-americans-especially-for-millennials/

Jamie Ducharme, "More Millennials Are Dying 'Deaths of Despair,' as Overdose and Suicide Rates Climb," TIME, accessed May 3, 2019, https://time.com/5606411/millennials-deaths-of-despair/

#8 Where We Are Today

Elaine K. Howley, What Mental Health Statistics Can Tell Us," U.S. News, accessed June 26, 2019, https://health.usnews.com/conditions/mental-health/articles/what-mental-health-statistics-can-tell-us

Jean M. Twenge, Bell A. Cooper, Thomas E. Joiner, Mary E. Duffy, & Sarah G. Binau, "Age, period, and cohort trends in mood disorder indicators and suicide-related outcomes in a nationally representative dataset, 2005-2017.", Journal of Abnormal Psychology, Vol 128(3), Apr 2019, 185-199, American Psychological Association, https://psycnet.apa.org/doiLanding?doi=10.1037%2Fabn0000410

Pew Research Center, "Religious Landscape Study," accessed June 26, 2019, https://www.pewforum.org/religious-landscape-study/generational-cohort/younger-millennial/

Rebecca Ayer, "Chronic loneliness in older adults leads to more doctors' office visits, UGA study finds," UGA Today, accessed June 17, 2019, https://news.uga.edu/chronic-loneliness-older-adults-more-doctors-office-visits-0315/

King's College London, "Depressed, inactive and out of work – study reveals lives of lonely young adults," accessed June 17, 2019, https://www.kcl.ac.uk/ioppn/news/records/2018/april/depressed-inactive-and-out-of-work--study-reveals-lives-of-lonely-young-adults (https://www.kcl.ac.uk/ioppn/news/records/2018/april/depressed-inactive-and-out-of-work-%E2%80%93-study-reveals-lives-of-lonely-young-adults)

Kristie Auman-Bauer, "Research explores kinless population of older adults in the U.S.," Penn State News, accessed June 18, 2019, https://news.psu.edu/story/486014/2017/10/12/research/research-explores-kinless-population-older-adults-us

Ipsos, "Over Half of Americans Report Feeling Like No One Knows Them Well," accessed June 19, 2019, https://www.ipsos.com/en-us/news-polls/us-loneliness-index-report

Quora, "Loneliness Might Be A Bigger Health Risk Than Smoking Or Obesity," Forbes, accessed June 19, 2019, https://www.forbes.com/sites/quora/2017/01/18/loneliness-might-be-a-bigger-health-risk-than-smoking-or-obesity/#6d4e1cde25d1

Anxiety and Depression Association of America, "About ADAA: Facts and Statistics," accessed June 26, 2019, https://adaa.org/about-adaa/press-room/facts-statistics

Daniel Steingold, "Survey: Most Millennials, Gen Z Adults Prefer Texting Over Talking In Person," StudyFinds, accessed June 26, 2019, https://www.studyfinds.org/millennials-gen-z-communicate-texting/

Jean Twenge, "With teen mental health deteriorating over five years, there's a likely culprit," The Conversation, accessed June 26, 2019, https://theconversation.com/with-teen-mental-health-deteriorating-over-five-years-theres-a-likely-culprit-86996

Aaron Smith & Monica Anderson, "Social Media Use in 2018," Pew Research Center, accessed June 27, 2019, https://www.pewinternet.org/2018/03/01/social-media-use-in-2018/

Katie Reilly, "Record Numbers of College Students Are Seeking Treatment for Depression and Anxiety – But Schools Can't Keep Up," TIME, accessed May 3, 2019, https://time.com/5190291/anxiety-depression-college-university-students/

Penn State Center for Collegiate Mental Health, "2016 Annual Report," accessed May 3, 2019, https://ccmh.psu.edu/files/2017/01/2016-Annual-Report-FINAL_2016_01_09-1gc2hj6.pdf

Pew Research Center, "Political Polarization in the American Public," accessed May 3, 2019, https://www.people-press.org/2014/06/12/political-polarization-in-the-american-public/

Rabah Kamal, "What are the current costs and outcomes related to mental health and substance use disorders?" Peterson-Kaiser Health System Tracker, accessed June 4, 2019, https://www.healthsystemtracker.